Be a TOP SCORER
in ISC Exams 2025

i Succeed

10 Sample Question Papers

with Quick Study Notes

Literature in English 12th

Paper 2

arihant
SUCCESS AND NOTHING LESS

Be a TOP SCORER
in ISC Exams 2025

i Succeed

10 Sample Question Papers

with Quick Study Notes

Literature in English 12th

Paper 2

AUTHOR
Chetansi Sharma

List of *iSucceed* Sample Papers for ISC 12

- Physics
- Chemistry
- Mathematics
- Biology
- Accounts
- Economics
- Commerce
- English Language
- Literature in English

Arihant Prakashan
(School Division Series)

Administrative & Production Offices

Regd. Office
'Ramchhaya' 4577/15, Agarwal Road, Darya Ganj, New Delhi -110002
Tele: 011- 47630600, 43518550

Head Office
Kalindi, TP Nagar, Meerut (UP) - 250002
Tel: 0121-7156203, 7156204

Sales & Support Offices
Agra, Ahmedabad, Bengaluru, Bareilly, Chennai, Delhi, Guwahati, Hyderabad, Jaipur, Jhansi, Kolkata, Lucknow, Nagpur & Pune.

PRICE ₹175.00

PO No : TXT-XX-XXXXXXX-X-XX

Published by Arihant Publications (India) Ltd.

For further information about the books published by Arihant, log on to www.arihantbooks.com or e-mail at info@arihantbooks.com

Follow us on

iSucceed

SAMPLE QUESTION PAPERS

THE **BEST CHOICE** OF TEACHERS & STUDENTS, Why?

01 Exact Exam Pattern

All Sample Papers have been designed on the actual exam format of ISC

02 Complete Syllabus

Complete coverage of syllabus through different types of questions across all the sample papers

03 Latest Specimen Question Paper

Latest Specimen Question Paper with detailed answers.

04 Detailed Answers

Step-by-step answers to help you understand concepts and improve problem-solving skills.

05 Quick Study Notes

Focused revision of the whole syllabus through Quick Study Notes.

06 All Type of Question

Coverage of all type of exam pattern questions, recall, analysis, understanding, application & evaluation

With Free DOUBT SOLVING APP

Free Doubt Solving APP

To help you sort out your doubts at any time any place.

***i*Succeed**

Literature in English Class 12

Course Structure
2024-25

Literature in English (Prescribed Texts)

Candidates will be required to answer questions based on the prescribed textbooks, which include Drama, Prose (Short Stories) and Poetry.

Drama and Prose (Short Stories) Questions set will be central to the text. Candidates will be required to show that they have understood the questions asked and are able to clearly respond in their own words. Questions will test understanding, appreciation and ability to analyse and synthesise.

Poetry Questions on a poem or a group of poems will be set to test the candidates' response. The questions will focus on the content, understanding and the personal response of candidates to the entire poem. Candidates' ability to appreciate content, stylistic and literary features of the poem(s) in question will also be tested.

Syllabus to be Covered

I. **DRAMA:**

Macbeth: William Shakespeare (Acts III, IV & V)

II. **PRISM: A Collection of ISC Short Stories** (Evergreen Publications (India) Ltd. New Delhi)

1. Atithi / Guest – Rabindranath Tagore
2. The Cookie Lady – Philip K. Dick
3. There Will Come Soft Rains – Ray Bradbury
4. Indigo – Satyajit Ray
5. The Medicine Bag – Virginia Driving Hawk Sneve

III. **RHAPSODY: A Collection of ISC Poems** (Evergreen Publications (India) Ltd. New Delhi)

1. Telephone Conversation – Wole Soyinka
2. Tithonus – Alfred, Lord Tennyson
3. Beethoven – Shane Koyczan
4. Small Towns and the River – Mamang Dai
5. Death be not Proud – John Donne

NOTE: The ISC (Class XII) Examination paper will be set ONLY on the portion of the syllabus that is prescribed for Class XII.

Preparation Assessment Zone

Welcome to the Preparation Assessment Zone !

In this section, you'll find **ISC Specimen Paper** to help you assess your readiness. Attempt these papers to familiarise yourself with the exam format and identify areas that need improvement.

Progress Tracker **Tick the papers as you complete them.**

☐ ISC Specimen Paper

ISC Specimen Paper

Session 2024-25

Literature in English 12th (Code 801)

Class 12

General Instructions

1. It has 5 questions in all.
2. Answer all questions.
3. While answering Question 1 in Section A, you are required to write only ONE option as the correct answer.
4. Internal choice has been given in the long answer questions on Drama, Prose and Poetry.
5. Do not exceed the prescribed word limit while answering the questions in Section B.
6. The intended marks for questions are given in brackets [ ].

- No. of Questions : 5
- No. of Sections : 2
- Time Alloted : 3 Hrs.
- Max. Marks : 80

Section A *(20 Marks)*

Question 1.

Choose the correct option for the following questions. **(10)**

(i) How does Lady Macbeth attempt to divert the attention of the guests from Macbeth's strange behaviour at the banquet? **[Recall]**

(a) She uses her social grace and charm to distract the guests.
(b) She engages the guests in conversation and entertainment.
(c) She pretends that Macbeth has an illness that is momentary.
(d) She speaks of Macbeth's courage in troubled times.

(ii) What is Macbeth's reaction when he sees Banquo's ghost at the banquet? **[Recall]**

(a) He pretends to remain calm and collected.
(b) He is terrified and loses control over himself.
(c) He blames Ross and Lennox for playing tricks on him.
(d) He is proud and boastful.

(iii) What does Banquo's soliloquy in Act III Scene 1 of the play *Macbeth* reveal about him? **[Understanding]**

(a) He is afraid of Macbeth.
(b) He is puzzled and confused.
(c) He is jealous of Macbeth and wishes to seize the throne.
(d) He is suspicious of Macbeth's actions.

(iv) In Act V of the play *Macbeth*, which one of the following do you think reflects the tragic arc of the play? [Analysis]

(P) Macbeth's soliloquy; Out, out brief candle, Life's but a walking shadow.

(Q) Lady Macbeth's breakdown: What's done cannot be undone.

(R) Macduff's greeting: Hail, King of Scotland.

(S) Malcolm's final words: So, thanks to all at once and to each one, whom we invite to see us crowned at Scone.

(a) (P) and (R) (b) (P) and (Q)

(c) (R) and (S) (d) (P) and (S)

(v) Read the two statements from the short story 'The Cookie Lady' and choose the correct option from the ones given below. [Analysis]

Statement I Why don't you read to me from your books? You know I don't see too well anymore and it's comfort to me to be read to.

Statement II You don't mind if I touch your arm, do you?

(a) Statement I and II are similar.

(b) Statement I and II are not related to each other.

(c) Statement II is the reason for Statement I.

(d) Statement I is the reason for Statement II.

(vi) Which of the following BEST captures the central idea of the short story 'The Medicine Bag'? [Interpret]

(a) Embracing one's cultural roots. (b) Disrespect for the older generation.

(c) The fruits of modernisation. (d) Peer pressure in adolescent.

(vii) Which natural element plays a crucial role in the end of the story 'There Will Come Soft Rains'? [Recall]

(a) Hail (b) Wind

(c) Heat (d) Rain

(viii) In the poem 'Telephone Conversation', the potent metaphor "stench of rancid breath" is used to [Interpret]

(a) evoke a strong sense of repulsion and disgust.

(b) describe bad odour in the telephone booth.

(c) create a toxic atmosphere.

(d) create a mental image of the lady with bad breath.

(ix) Why does Shane Koyczan begin the poem 'Beethoven' with the word 'Listen'? [Analysis]

(a) To highlight the fact that Beethoven was abused.

(b) To make the poem appealing and lend rhythm.

(c) To add novelty to the beginning.

(d) To align it with the theme of music.

(x) How is Death personified in the opening lines of the poem 'Death Be Not Proud'? [Recall]

(a) As a desperate man (b) As a gentle agent of Fate

(c) As a mighty conqueror (d) As a reaper of souls

Question 2.

Complete the following sentences by providing a reason for each in brief. Do not write the question. (10)

(i) Macbeth returns to the witches in Act IV Scene 1 because .... [Understanding]

(ii) In Act V Scene 8 of the play *Macbeth*, Macbeth initially refuses to fight Macduff because .... [Recall]

(iii) In Act III Scene 4 of the play *Macbeth*, Lady Macbeth dismissed the guests at the banquet without standing on any ceremony because......... . [Analysis]

(iv) The escape of Fleance in Act III Scene 3 of the play *Macbeth* is significant because .... [Interpret]

(v) In the short story 'Atithi', Motilal Babu and Annapurna choose Tarapada as a prospective groom for their daughter because......... . [Recall]

(vi) In the short story 'The Cookie Lady', Mrs. Drew wanted Bubber to keep visiting her because .... [Understanding]

(vii) In the short story 'Indigo', Aniruddha asked Sukhanram if there were ghosts in the bungalow because......... . [Recall]

(viii) In the poem 'Telephone Conversation', the speaker resented the landlady asking him about the colour of his skin because .... [Analysis]

(ix) In the poem 'Small Towns and the River', the dead are placed pointing West because .... [Recall]

(x) Beethoven amputated the legs of his piano because .... [Recall]

Section B *(60 Marks)*

Macbeth-William Shakespeare

Question 3.

(i) How does Malcolm's character grow and change over the course of the play? Incorporate the following details and write your answer in a short paragraph of about 100-150 words. [Analysis] (5)

(a) Malcolm's testing of Macduff in Act IV

(b) His generalship and the restoration of order through Macduff

(ii) In what ways does power corrupt in the play *Macbeth*? Discuss any one character who is corrupted by power in the play. Incorporate the following details and answer in 100-150 words. [Understanding] (5)

(a) The character's traits before coming to power

(b) The character's degeneration after coming into power

(iii) (a) Do you agree with the view that Macbeth is fighting a lost battle against forces beyond his control? Justify your point of view in about 200-250 words by referring to the Acts studied. [Evaluate] (10)

Or

(b) When do you have flashes of sympathy and admiration for Lady Macbeth in the course of the play? Explain by citing examples from the Acts studied. Write your answer in about 200-250 words. [Interpret]

Prism-A Collection of Short Stories

Question 4.

(i) 'The Medicine Bag' traces the narrator's attitude to his Sioux Grandfather from mild embarrassment to appreciation. Summarise the reasons for this embarrassment and the change.
Write your answer in 100-150 words incorporating the following details. [Understanding](5)

(a) Reasons for embarrassment

(b) Specific reasons for the change in attitude

(ii) Referring closely to the short story 'The Cookie Lady', explore Mrs. Drew's fascination with Bubber. Answer in 100-150 words Incorporating the following details. [Understanding](5)

(a) Mrs. Drew's repeated interactions with Bubber

(b) Role of the cookies in the short story

(iii) (a) Tarapada, the central character in the short story 'Atithi' is a free soul who cannot be restrained by the bonds of society. Examine this statement in 200-250 words. [Analysis](10)

Or

(b) Discuss the absence of human characters in the story 'There Will Come Soft Rains'. How does this absence contribute to the overall tone and message of the narrative? Answer in 200-250 words. [Analysis]

Rhapsody-Poetry

Question 5.

(i) In what ways does the speaker's cultural background clash with the landlady's expectations in the poem 'Telephone Conversation'? [Understanding](5)
Write your answer in 100-150 words incorporating the following details.
(a) The speaker's conversation with the landlady
(b) The undertones of racial and colour bias in the conversation

(ii) Referring to the poem 'Tithonus', show how his immortality becomes a curse. Answer in 100-150 words incorporating the following details. [Understanding](5)
(a) Circumstances leading to Tithonus receiving a boon
(b) Reasons for the boon becoming a curse

(iii) (a) Analyse the comparison between death and sleep in the poem 'Death Be Not Proud'. How does this metaphor contribute to the overall message of the sonnet? Write your answer in about 200-250 words. [Analysis] (10)

Or

(b) The poem 'Beethoven' explores the role of pain and suffering in the process of artistic creativity and excellence. Justify this statement in 200-250 words. [Evaluate]

Answers *in Topper's Style*

1. (i) (c) She pretends that Macbeth has an illness that is momentary.
(ii) (b) He is terrified and loses control over himself.
(iii) (d) He is suspicious of Macbeth's actions.
(iv) (b) (P) and (Q)
(v) (d) Statement I is the reason for Statement II.
(vi) (a) Embracing one's cultural roots.
(vii) (b) Wind
(viii) (a) evoke a strong sense of repulsion and disgust.
(ix) (d) To align it with the theme of music.
(x) (c) As a mighty conqueror

2. (i) he is increasingly desperate and wants reassurance about his future
(ii) he was already burdened with guilt of the murders he had committed
(iii) she recognised signs of Macbeth's troubled mind and was afraid that he may spill the truth and make a fool of himself
(iv) it ensures that Banquo's line could potentially survive, fulfilling the prophecy that Banquo's descendants would inherit the throne
(v) she was their only daughter and so would be able to stay with them even after marriage
(vi) she drew from his vitality and enjoyed the transformation she experienced
(vii) the place was spooky and old dak bungalows had a reputation for being haunted
(viii) being judged on the basis of skin colour was ignorant and insulting for the speaker
(ix) when the soul rises, it will walk towards the East toward heaven
(x) he was deaf and got down on his knees so that he could feel the vibrations of the music he played through the floor

3. (i) In William Shakespeare's play *Macbeth*, Malcolm, the eldest son of King Duncan, undergoes a significant transformation. Initially, weak, inexperienced and fearful of getting killed, he flees Scotland after his father's murder. However, as the play progresses, we can see that Malcolm matures. With the help of Macduff and the English army, he eventually overthrows Macbeth, retakes the throne and restores the order that was shattered when Duncan was killed. Malcolm represents stability and lawfulness which is in contrast with Macbeth's violent ambitions and apathy towards his people. His determination to avenge Duncan's death and reclaim the rightful throne underscores his commitment to Scotland's well-being and contrasts sharply with Macbeth's bloodthirsty pursuit of power.

(ii) In the play, the best example of corruption by power is displayed by Macbeth. He is an important character in the play as the title suggests. Macbeth, who was initially a valiant and loyal general to King Duncan, after being manipulated by the Three Witches and his own wife, Lady Macbeth, murders Duncan and usurps the throne. Macbeth's initial murder, the murder of King Duncan, sets the stage for his descent into guilt-ridden madness. The blood on his hands becomes a metaphor for the weight of his crimes. His hallucinations, like the ghostly appearance of Banquo, reveal his inner turmoil and torment.

As he gains power by becoming the king, he loses his peace and remains in constant fear of losing the throne. He even becomes lonelier due to his paranoia and starts facing a protest against his tyranny from his own people. This leaves him isolated, anxious and consumed with guilt; thus reflecting the degeneration of his character.

(iii) (a) Yes, I agree with the view that Macbeth is fighting a lost battle against forces beyond his control. Although Macbeth's downfall was caused by his own choices, there were still forces that drove him close to his death and he couldn't have influenced them.

The first instance of this is the seed of ambition that was planted in his consciousness by the witches' prophecies and further grown into a disaster by Lady Macbeth's manipulation. Lady Macbeth was also an ambitious lady and hence wanted her husband to be the King of Scotland. She greatly influenced Macbeth's actions and led him to his destruction. Later on, he was misguided by the apparitions shown by the witches which made him believe he could change his fate. In his hunger for power and anxiety to secure himself against the enemies or potential threats to his kingship, he killed innocent people, like Banquo and Macduff's family. Although these choices were made by him, we can't say he consciously made the decisions as he was driven by his ambitions and fear.

It is evident from his soliloquies, that he was going through a struggle within which led him to make wrong choices. For example, in his soliloquy in Act III, he muses on Banquo and reflects that he is the only one in the kingdom who he's scared of. Unlike Banquo, he couldn't suppress his ambition of gaining the throne as his ambitiousness was fueled by his wife and the witches. Thus, trusting others resulted in Macbeth's eventual downfall.

(b) Lady Macbeth's character is complex and deserves the readers' sympathy and admiration. Looking at the play from the point of view of the readers of the time, i.e. the Elizabethan era, female characters in literature were not expected to be brave or ambitious like Lady Macbeth. The admiration for Lady Macbeth arises when she's seen being brave and behaving calmly during the banquet when Macbeth almost loses his mind. Lady Macbeth stabilises her husband and also manages the situation by averting the guests' attention. She is also seen to be strategic in her approach and appears as a strong partner to Macbeth as she not only supports him but also guides him when needed.

Lady Macbeth is as much capable of expressing herself as she is of hiding her true self. For instance, in Act III before the banquet, she shares her concerns with Macbeth and expresses her inner turmoil while also taking care of Macbeth. However, readers must also sympathise with her because whatever dark deeds she did and was a part of was all for fulfilling her husband's ambition and to see him succeed like a dutiful wife. Despite her efforts to help Macbeth achieve his goal, when Macbeth gains power, he distances himself from her, ultimately leaving her alone with immense guilt and a deteriorating psyche. Lady Macbeth eventually dies due to her inner turmoil that consumes her which shows she regretted her actions and was not innately evil.

4. (i) Martin's character develops from being embarrassed of his Grandpa's appearance that does not match the popular standards and the image of Indians on the tv to embracing his heritage and culture wholeheartedly.

Like many kids his age, Martin prioritises popularity and social acceptance from his peers. He avoids anything that might disrupt this carefully curated image of his Sioux grandfather. Initially, he resents his grandfather's presence fearing that it will interfere with his modern city-identity. However, as the story progresses, we see Martin slowly embracing his culture and his hesitation and fear of his friends meeting his Grandpa vanishing. Martin initially avoids his friends from coming to visit his grandfather but, one day, when they follow him home, Grandpa puts on his best beaded vest and his favourite moccasins. Martin feels ashamed of his own feelings as his friends are impressed by his Grandpa's attitude and his warm demeanour and they do not mock him for being exotic like Martin had envisioned. Later on, when Grandpa explains the history and significance of the medicine bag to him, he feels proud of his roots. Ultimately, Martin accepts his mixed identity with love and respect.

(ii) As per the story 'The Cookie Lady', Mrs. Drew was an elderly lady who lived alone in her house. Although she had an eerie presence about her and was known as the 'creepy old lady' in the neighbourhood, her demeanour around Bubber appears to be kind and warm. Mrs. Drew was lonely and had no one to interact with so she decided to lure Bubber into her house by baking fresh cookies and offering them to him when he passed by her house. Bubber, being a child, loved cookies and easily fell for Mrs. Drew's trick. Whenever Bubber visited, she would bake him fresh cookies and offer them to him with a glass of milk. She would ask him to read to him to spend more time in his company. Her intentions, however, were evil as, whenever Bubber sat near Mrs. Drew reading out from his school books, she began to change supernaturally into a beautiful young woman. Eventually, she sucked all of Bubber's vitality and youth when he informed her that he wouldn't be visiting her anymore. Hence, Bubber's greed for cookies became the reason for his tragic end.

(iii) (a) Tarapada, the main character of the story 'Atithi', was a wandering Brahmin boy. He was the fourth son of his family but was still loved dearly by his family and the entire village. He had a charismatic appearance and could make anyone like him just by interacting with them once. Even though he was a darling to everyone, this little boy left his hometown by accompanying a touring jatra-troupe without thinking twice.

Although he was brought back home by the search parties employed by his family, they still couldn't keep him at home for long. Tarapada could not accept any kind of ties or bonds even if they were bonds of love. He was free spirited and had a deep longing for exploration. From a very young age, Tarapada had a depth in his character and could appreciate finer things in life like a grown person. He loved music and nature deeply and, therefore, soon joined a group of Panchali singers and learned to sing from their leader. However, the leader of the group began to treat Tarapada as his own son and, therefore, he left them too without notice.

He kept moving from one place to another, with a detached attitude, learning new skills, appreciating nature and not remembering the dreadful sights that he saw. All these instances from the story show that Tarapada truly is a free soul who cannot be restrained by the bonds of society.

(b) In Ray Bradbury's science fiction short story 'There Will Come Soft Rains', several literary devices highlight the theme of humanity's insignificance in the face of technological advancement and destruction. The story lacks any living human characters which emphasises their absence. The house, which is an automated relic, becomes the central character continuing its routines despite the vanished inhabitants. This absence highlights the eerie emptiness and the irreversible impact of an atomic catastrophe. In the absence of any human characters in the story, the house and its components take the centre stage. The house has a 'brain' which is the attic where the software system of the automated house is set up, and it reads out reminders and alarms through its walls.

There are mice that clean the house and even seem to show the emotion of 'anger' when a dog enters spreading mud around making their job of keeping the house clean difficult. It is chilling to note that there is no human presence but the work assigned by them is still carried out effortlessly by the machines they've made. Time, which is a human construct, still exists in the house which reflects the irony in the story. At last, the wind, an element of nature, becomes the cause of destruction for the mechanised house. There are still trees, birds, foxes, cats and dogs at the end of the story which implies that nature may thrive again even when humans have vanished.

5. (i) In the poem 'Telephone Conversation', the speaker is an African black man while the landlady is a British white woman. During their telephonic interaction, the landlady asks the speaker about his skin colour as she is racially biased and does not want to rent her apartment out to a black person despite her claims of being non-discriminatory in the ad that she had put out. Under the fabric of politeness, the landlady tries to hide her colour bias but fails as, when she questions the speaker, he responds with 'dark' to which she replies 'how dark?'. This shocks and confuses the speaker and, after a moment of silence, he decides to give the lady a taste of her own absurdity by naming the colour of each part of his body. He very cleverly drives the conversation from an upsetting interaction with hints of racial discrimination to a lesson to the landlady highlighting her ridiculousness.

(ii) 'Tithonus', a dramatic monologue by Alfred, Lord Tennyson, explores the consequences of immortality. The poem centres on Tithonus, a mortal man who was granted eternal life by the goddess Aurora (Eos). However, this divine gift turns into a curse, leading Tithonus to express profound regret.

Tithonus begins by reminiscing about his past—a time when he was chosen by Aurora as her lover. His beauty once rivalled that of the gods but now he is a mere shadow of his former self because, when he asked Aurora for the gift of immortality so that he could be with her forever, he did not know that he would continue to age while she would remain the same. The phrases 'falling woods' and 'weeping vapours' in the poem symbolise decay emphasising the relentless erosion of his mortal beauty. Therefore, immortality has cursed him by robbing him of vitality, leaving him trapped in perpetual ageing.

(iii) (a) In the poem 'Death Be Not Proud', the poet masterfully emphasises the powerlessness of death through various linguistic devices and a striking comparison with 'sleep'. Donne personifies death addressing it directly as if it were a conscious being. By calling it 'mighty and dreadful', he mocks its supposed authority. This personification reveals the limitations and vulnerability of death. The comparison of death to 'rest and sleep' is a powerful metaphor. Donne suggests that death is merely a transition, a temporary state that is similar to a restful sleep. The word 'pictures' implies that death's fearsome reputation is an illusion, and what lies beyond is familiar and comforting. The poet even suggests that drugs can induce a similar experience diminishing death's terror. The poet asserts that death is merely a slave to kings as their authority gives them the power to command death to take lives.

The poem concludes with the paradoxical statement: 'And death shall be no more; Death, thou shalt die'. This paradox lies in the contradiction that, if death dies, it cannot continue to exist. The very concept of death 'ceasing to be' contradicts its nature. Symbolically, it suggests that death, despite its apparent power, ultimately loses its dominion. According to the poet, eternal life transcends death, rendering death powerless.

In conclusion, Donne's defiance against death lies in portraying it as a mere interlude before the soul's eternal awakening .

(b) The poem 'Beethoven' by Shane Koyczan highlights how Beethoven's pain and suffering influenced his musical compositions. The poem delves into his struggle with deafness, a cruel irony for a composer whose life revolved around sound. This adversity is portrayed as both a source of deep despair and a catalyst for extraordinary creativity compelling him to compose by feeling and internal hearing rather than external sound.

Beethoven, the iconic composer, suffered both physically and emotionally, unable to find love within the confines of his home. His father's abusive behaviour left scars that ran deep, making it challenging for him to connect with others. Therefore, he sought solace in his music which for him is a refuge where he could express the inexpressible. Despite his deafness, he transformed emotion into symphonies creating a language that transcended mere notes. Koyczan's portrayal emphasises that, to truly understand Beethoven, one must listen to his compositions for they reveal the depths of his soul and the universal power of love.

Beethoven also struggled with the idea of perfectionism as his father never praised him. His father wanted him to be a musical genius, for which he pushed him hard and no matter how well he played, it was always "Not good enough".

To conclude, to cope with all the pain and sufferings in life, Beethoven turned to his music. He composed heartfelt symphonies as if music was his only outlet to express what he couldn't say through words.

Proficiency Building Zone

Welcome to the Proficiency Building Zone !

This section contains **10 Sample Question Papers** designed to enhance your problem-solving skills and proficiency. Use these papers to practice regularly and track your progress. Remember, consistent practice is key to mastering Literature in English.

Progress Tracker **Tick the papers as you complete them.**

- ☐ Sample Paper 1 _____ (Fill your score)
- ☐ Sample Paper 2 _____ (Fill your score)
- ☐ Sample Paper 3 _____ (Fill your score)
- ☐ Sample Paper 4 _____ (Fill your score)
- ☐ Sample Paper 5 _____ (Fill your score)
- ☐ Sample Paper 6 _____ (Fill your score)
- ☐ Sample Paper 7 _____ (Fill your score)
- ☐ Sample Paper 8 _____ (Fill your score)
- ☐ Sample Paper 9 _____ (Fill your score)
- ☐ Sample Paper 10 _____ (Fill your score)

SQP Code : **PB-1/10** Series ***i*-Succeed 1-25/10** Roll No. | | | | | | | | |

Sample Question Paper 01

Literature in English 12th (Code 801)

General Instructions

1. It has 5 questions in all.
2. Answer all questions.
3. While answering Question 1 in Section A, you are required to write only ONE option as the correct answer.
4. Internal choice has been given in the long answer questions on Drama, Prose and Poetry.
5. Do not exceed the prescribed word limit while answering the questions in Section B.
6. The intended marks for questions are given in brackets [ ].

Time : 3 Hrs.

Max. Marks : 80

Section A *(20 Marks)*

Question 1.

Choose the correct option for the following questions. (10)

(i) What does the consequence of Macbeth's attempt to influence fate by murdering Banquo and Fleance indicate? [Understanding]

(a) He successfully changes his future with his efforts
(b) The Witches' prophecy proves to be a trick
(c) In his efforts to control fate, he ends up sealing his own ruin
(d) He experienced success for a while but could not keep a hold on it

(ii) Why does Macbeth fear Banquo and his son Fleance? [Analysis]

(a) They are powerful warriors
(b) They are suspicious of Macbeth for Duncan's murder
(c) They were to assume the throne as per the prophecy
(d) They were out to get Macbeth

(iii) What is the outcome of the murder attempt on Banquo and Fleance? [Recall]

(a) Both Banquo and Fleance are killed
(b) Both Banquo and Fleance escape
(c) Banquo is killed but Fleance escapes
(d) Banquo escapes but Fleance is killed

(iv) Which of the following statements from the play reflects 'fear' as Macbeth's emotion? [Analysis]

(P) His words to the witches, 'I don't care if you unleash violent winds that tear down churches...'

(Q) His soliloquy, 'Out, out brief candle, Life's but a walking shadow!'

(R) Macbeth goes to the witches again to know more of his fate

(S) Macbeth hires murderers to kill Banquo and his son

(a) (P) and (Q)
(b) (Q) and (S)
(c) (P), (R) and (S)
(d) (Q) and (R)

(v) Read the two statements from the short story 'The Cookie Lady' and choose the correct option from the ones given below. [Analysis]

Statement I 'He sure is going to get a licking when he gets home'.

Statement II 'Listen! Do you hear something'?

(a) Statement I and II are similar.
(b) Statement I and II are not related to each other.
(c) Statement II is the reason for Statement I.
(d) Statement I is the reason for Statement II.

(vi) Why did the house play the poem 'There Will Come Soft Rains' in the story 'There Will Come Soft Rains'? [Understanding]

(a) It was Mrs. McClellan's favourite poem
(b) It was children's favourite poem
(c) It was randomly picked by the system
(d) It was everyone's favourite

(vii) What object does the statement 'Man, that really made an impression' refer to in the story 'The Medicine Bag'? [Recall]

(a) The pebbles
(b) The drum
(c) The shells
(d) The beaded shirt

(viii) The central idea of the poem 'Telephone Conversation' is [Interpret]

(a) romance
(b) prejudice and racial discrimination
(c) cultural identity crisis
(d) social class differences

SP-01

(ix) What do you infer about Beethoven's character from the statement: 'The man got down on his knees for no one'? [Understanding]

(a) He was a proud and arrogant man
(b) He was egoistic and selfish
(c) He had a high regard for his own values
(d) He was indifferent to society

(x) Which literary device has been used in the line 'And death shall be no more; death thou shalt die.' in the poem 'Death Be Not Proud'? [Understanding]

(a) Alliteration
(b) Euphemism
(c) Paradox
(d) Imagery

Question 2.

Complete the following sentences by providing a reason for each in brief. Do not write the question. (10)

(i) Macbeth initially refuses to fight Macduff in Act V Scene 6 of play *Macbeth* because .... [Understanding]

(ii) Duncan's sons flee after he is murdered because .... [Analysis]

(iii) Macbeth visits the three witches again because .... [Analysis]

(iv) In the play, *Macbeth,* Shakespeare highlights that Banquo too was ambitious because .... [Understanding]

(v) In the short story 'Atithi', Charushashi did not let Sonamani meet Tarapada because .... [Recall]

(vi) In the story 'The Cookie Lady', Bubber keeps visiting Mrs. Drew because .... [Interpret]

(vii) Aniruddha, in the story 'Indigo', had to stay in the Dak Bungalow because .... [Recall]

(viii) In the poem 'Telephone Conversation', the speaker did not wish to answer the landlady's question because .... [Understanding]

(ix) The rituals are viewed as permanent by the poet, in the poem 'Small towns and the river' because .... [Recall]

(x) Beethoven could transfer his emotions into music because .... [Analysis]

Section B *(60 Marks)*

Macbeth–William Shakespeare

Question 3.

(i) Why do you think Banquo is initially sceptical of the witches? Comment in 100-150 words including following details. [Analysis] (5)

(a) Change in Banquo's thoughts about the prophecies in Act III

(b) Banquo's suspicion on Macbeth

(ii) Describe the mood established at the beginning of Act IV, Scene 1 of the play *Macbeth*. What elements contribute to this eerie atmosphere? Give your answer in 100-150 words incorporating following details. [Understanding] (5)

(a) Main characters of Act IV Scene 1

(b) The significance of this scene in the play

(iii) (a) Are the witches in the play *Macbeth* real? What effect do their prophecies have on Macbeth's actions? Explain by citing examples from the Acts studied. Write your answer in about 200-250 words. [Interpret] (10)

Or

(b) By citing examples, explain the significance of Lady Macbeth's role in the play. Give your answer in 200-250 words. [Evaluate]

Prism–A Collection of Short Stories

Question 4.

(i) In the story 'The Medicine bag', Grandpa wants to give the medicine bag to Martin. Discuss Martin's reaction to this in 100-150 words. Incorporate the following details [Evaluate] (5)

(a) Martin's initial feelings on receiving this unusual inheritance

(b) His acceptance of the medicine bag

(ii) Why did Mrs. Drew want Bubber to keep visiting her? With reference to the story 'The Cookie Lady', answer this question in 100-150 words including the following details. [Analysis] (5)

(a) Mrs. Drew's character in the story

(b) Bubber's motivation to visit Mrs. Drew

(iii) (a) From the short story 'Atithi', discuss Charushashi and Tarapada's relationship commenting on their initial interactions versus the later developments with some examples. Give your answer in 200-250 words. [Analysis] (10)

Or

(b) How is the tone and the narrative affected by the absence of human characters in the story 'There Will Come Soft Rains'? Discuss in 200-250 words. [Interpret]

Rhapsody-Poetry

Question 5.

(i) With the reference to the poem 'Telephone Conversation', discuss how the speaker's tone changes as the lady enquires about his skin colour. Why does it affect the speaker? Give your answer in 100-150 words incorporating the following details [Understanding] (5)

(a) The speaker's clever response to the question

(b) Highlight of the poem

(ii) Based on the poem, comment on Tithonus' emotions towards immortality including the following details. Give your answer in 100-150 words. [Analysis] (5)

(a) Tithonus' feelings about immortality

(b) The changes in his feelings later

(iii) (a) Beethoven's pain and suffering translates into music, and music becomes his creative outlet. Discuss the given statement in 200-250 words. [Evaluate] (10)

Or

(b) Based on the poem 'Death Be Not Proud', what can you say about the poet's faith? Discuss in 200-250 words. [Evaluate]

Answers in Topper's Style

1. (i) (b) The Witches' prophecy proves to be a trick
   (ii) (c) They were to assume the throne as per the prophecy
   (iii) (c) Banquo is killed but Fleance escapes
   (iv) (c) (P), (R) and (S)
   (v) (b) Statement I and II are not related to each other
   (vi) (a) It was Mrs. McClellan's favourite poem
   (vii) (b) The drum
   (viii) (b) prejudice and racial discrimination
   (ix) (c) He had a high regard for his own values
   (x) (c) Paradox

2. (i) Macbeth had murdered Macduff's entire family, and this guilt weighs heavily on him
   (ii) they fear becoming the killer's next target
   (iii) his curiosity drives him to seek further insight into his fate, despite the ominous prophecies he has already received
   (iv) the writer wants to keep his characters real by emphasising their natural human tendencies and fallibilities
   (v) she did not want to share Tarapada's affection or attention with her friend
   (vi) she would offer him freshly baked cookies which he loved
   (vii) he encountered a thunderstorm during his journey, his car broke down in the middle of nowhere, and he needed food and shelter for the night
   (viii) of the racial prejudice he encountered during their conversation
   (ix) they persist despite the impermanence of human existence. The river, in contrast, flows eternally, symbolising continuity and permanence
   (x) music became the language through which he expressed his innermost feelings and struggles

3. (i) Banquo is sceptical of the Witches' intentions and remains unconvinced of the Witches' prophecy. Banquo warns Macbeth that 'instruments of darkness' often tell half-truths 'to win us to our harm. This shows his scepticism and initial thoughts on the prophecies given by the witches or 'weird sisters'. While the Witches had prophesied great futures for both Banquo and Macbeth, and Banquo wasn't convinced or intrigued and would rather leave the matter safely alone as he did not want to unnecessarily get involved and become greedy/ambitious.

   In Act III, Scene 1, Banquo's soliloquy reveals that he is suspicious of Macbeth, who, in becoming king, has achieved all that the Witches promised him. Banquo senses that Macbeth engaged in foul play in order to make the Witches' prophecy come true. While the idea that Macbeth may have murdered Duncan fills Banquo with fear, the thought also gives Banquo hope that what the Witches predicted for him will come true. However, he doesn't realise that in order for his sons to become king, he will have to eventually die.

   (ii) In Act IV, Scene 1 of *Macbeth,* the mood is undeniably eerie and foreboding. The scene unfolds in a cavern where the three witches, often referred to as the 'weird sisters', gather. Their presence alone contributes to the unsettling atmosphere. As they throw ingredients like 'eye of newt and toe of frog' into a boiling cauldron, their incantations create an otherworldly ambiance. Hecate, the goddess of witchcraft, joins them, and they all dance and sing. Macbeth then enters demanding answers from the witches.

   The significance of this scene lies in the prophecies the witches reveal to Macbeth. The three apparitions – the floating armed head warning him to beware Macduff, the bloody child assuring him that no man born of a woman can harm him, and the crowned child with a tree promising his invincibility – shape Macbeth's decisions and ultimately lead to his tragic downfall. The eerie setting and the witches' cryptic words foreshadow the chaos and bloodshed that occurs later in the play.

   (iii) (a) Yes, the witches in the play *Macbeth* are real. Macbeth sees the three Witches and converses with them which proves they weren't manifestations of his mind. Throughout the play, Banquo and Macbeth seem to embrace the Witches as real physical beings, despite Banquo's initial doubts about their existence and his thoughts on whether they were just hallucinations. The Witches attempted to cause havoc by prophesying to Macbeth in order to compel him to act.

   They sowed the seeds of evil in Macbeth's mind, which developed to rule his thoughts. However, it was Macbeth who took the decisions that sealed his doom as he wasn't forced to kill Duncan or any of his other victims. But, after murdering Duncan, Macbeth lost his sanity and this suggests that the Witches had been able to control his mind. Some examples from the play that prove this are as follows

In Act III, Scene 1, the Witches' initial prophecy—that Macbeth will be king—fuels his ambition. However, the parallel prophecy regarding Banquo's descendants disturbs him. Macbeth becomes obsessed with securing his lineage, leading him to order Banquo's murder. The Witches' words haunt him driving him toward ruthless acts. In Act III, Scene 3, Macbeth commissions murderers to kill Banquo and his son, Fleance. His obsession with the Witches' prophecy- specifically about Banquo's descendants—drives him to eliminate any threat.

The Witches' transform Macbeth into a ruthless villain who is willing to sacrifice friendship and innocence for power. In Act IV, Scene 1, the Witches conjure three apparitions for Macbeth. These visions, representing an armed head, a bloody child, and a crowned child with a tree, foretell his fate. The Witches' cryptic guidance fuels Macbeth's overconfidence and reckless decisions. He starts believing he is invincible leading to further bloodshed. In conclusion, the Witches' prophecies act as a malevolent force, goading Macbeth toward his tragic downfall. Their words manipulate his desires, distort his morality, and ultimately seal his fate.

(b) In the play *Macbeth,* Lady Macbeth emerges as a multifaceted character whose actions significantly impact the play's unfolding tragedy. In Act III, Lady Macbeth's relentless ambition drives her manipulation of her husband. She overrides his objections questioning his manhood until he commits murder to prove himself. Her strength of will persists even after Duncan's assassination, steadying Macbeth's nerves. Lady Macbeth embodies the theme of gender and power, challenging traditional roles by taking on a masculine assertiveness.

The Witches' prophecies haunt Lady Macbeth as seen in Act IV. Her guilt intensifies paralleling her pre-crime ambition.

The three apparitions—armed head, bloody child and crowned child foretell Macbeth's fate. Lady Macbeth's influence wanes as guilt plagues her more strongly and she becomes a tragic figure, unable to cope with the legacy of their crimes. In Act V, Lady Macbeth's sensitivity, once a strength, becomes her weakness.

Sleepwalking through the castle, she desperately tries to wash away an invisible bloodstain. Her mental breakdown mirrors her earlier ambition and she takes her own life, symbolising her inability to grapple with guilt and consequences. In summary, Lady Macbeth's character navigates ambition, manipulation, guilt, and madness, leaving an indelible mark on the play's tragic trajectory.

4. (i) In the short story 'The Medicine Bag', Martin's reaction to Grandpa's intention of passing down the sacred medicine bag is a blend of reverence, curiosity, and emotional conflict. Initially, Martin is deeply honoured by the gesture, recognising the bag's significance as a cherished family heirloom. The medicine bag symbolises cultural heritage, spiritual connection and ancestral wisdom. However, Martin's internal struggle emerges as he grapples with the weight of tradition and the responsibility that comes with it. His mixed emotions—awe, pride, and perhaps a touch of fear—highlight the tension between honouring the past and navigating his own identity in a modern world. Martin's acceptance of the medicine bag becomes a pivotal moment, signifying his willingness to embrace both his heritage and the challenges of bridging generational gaps.

(ii) In the short story 'The Cookie Lady' by Philip K. Dick, Mrs. Drew is portrayed as a lonely old widow who craves companionship. She lives a solitary life and has almost no company. Her isolation is palpable and, thus, she finds solace in the presence of Bernard 'Bubber' Surle, a young boy who visits her after school every day. Mrs. Drew's character is defined by her yearning for connection. As a consequence, she enjoys Bubber's visits immensely. Baking him cookies becomes a way for her to express affection and to create a bond with him. Bubber, on the other hand, is motivated by genuine kindness and empathy.

He recognises Mrs. Drew's loneliness and willingly spends time with her, reading to her after enjoying the cookies she bakes. His visits provide her with much-needed companionship and, in return, Mrs. Drew's transformation into a younger version of herself during one of these visits adds an eerie and mysterious dimension to the story.

(iii) (a) Charushashi and Tarapada had a complex relationship. It was marked by a blend of affection and antagonism. Initially, Charushashi dislikes and often resents Tarapada for the affection and attention that he receives from her parents. However, her feelings evolve indicating a deeper emotional connection. This relationship oscillates between moments of anger, jealousy and understanding, which reflects the refinement in dynamics of a love-hate relationship where emotions are often intense but contradictory.

Despite moments of jealousy and anger, overtime, Charushashi's understanding of Tarapada deepens and she recognises his restless spirit and eternal wanderlust. His mysterious disappearance on the day of his wedding reflects the tension between domesticity and the quest for freedom. Ultimately, Charushashi's perception of Tarapada transcends mere resentment, further revealing layers of empathy and complexity in their relationship.

One instance from the story that encapsulates this complexity is their conversation by the pond-

Charushashi, initially wary of Tarapada, begins to open up as she questions him about his wandering lifestyle, seeking to understand the root of his restlessness. Tarapada, in turn, responds with a mix of playfulness and vulnerability. He shares stories of his travels describing distant lands, exotic cultures, and the allure of the unknown. His eyes light up as he recounts adventures and Charushashi is drawn to this free-spirited man who defies convention. This exchange reveals layers of emotion between them.

As they part ways, Charushashi gazes at the ripples in the pond contemplating the choices before her. Tarapada's departure leaves her with a sense of loss but also a newfound courage to explore life beyond the familiar. Therefore, Tarapada becomes not only an atithi (guest) but also a catalyst for Charushashi's self-discovery.

(b) The story 'There Will Come Soft Rains' portrays a dystopian future where all of mankind has been destroyed and all that remains is its creations, more specifically the technology man has created. Even though the humans have vanished, their mechanised home still functions round the clock like it used to. The alarm goes off in the morning, the reminders are read out, the breakfast is cooked and served by the robotic kitchen and even the mice are artificial as they do their cleaning duties diligently. The nursery which once entertained children with high quality graphics and learning tools, now sings rhymes and displays lessons with no audience. It is chilling to note that there is no human presence but the work assigned by them is still carried out effortlessly by the machines they've made.

Time, which is a human construct, still exists in the house which reflects the irony in the story. Another example of such irony is portrayed in the lines, 'It quivered at each sound, the house did. If a sparrow brushed a window, the shade snapped up. The bird, startled, flew off! No, not even a bird must touch the house!'. The house that was designed to 'protect' couldn't really protect what it was made to. At last, the wind, an element of nature, becomes the cause of destruction for the mechanised house. There are still trees, birds, foxes, cats and dogs at the end of the story, implying that nature may, in time, thrive once again.

5. (i) In Wole Soyinka's poem 'Telephone Conversation', the speaker's tone undergoes a significant shift when the lady enquires about his skin colour. Initially, the speaker encounters silence in response to the stereotypical questions about their skin colour reflecting the racism prevalent at the time. As the lady presses further, demanding to know if the speaker is 'light' or 'dark,' his tone becomes more defensive and sarcastic.

The speaker cleverly responds by comparing his skin colour to 'sepia' and then to a mix of brunette and blonde, highlighting the absurdity of reducing human identity to simplistic categories. The lady's inquiry affects the speaker because it exposes her racial bias, forcing the speaker to navigate a discriminatory conversation. Thus, the poem highlights the casual racism that people of colour often encounter, emphasising the importance of addressing such biases in society.

(ii) In Alfred, Lord Tennyson's poem 'Tithonus', the character initially views immortality with a sense of awe and longing. As the lover of Aurora, the goddess of dawn, Tithonus desires eternal life to be with her forever. His initial feelings are marked by a romantic idealism, envisioning endless days filled with love and companionship. However, as time passes, Tithonus realises the harsh reality of immortality. He becomes trapped in an unending existence, ageing relentlessly while Aurora remains eternally youthful. Later, his feelings shift from longing to despair as he grapples with the monotony of endless days and the gradual decay of his body.

The poem poignantly portrays the tragic consequences of immortality emphasising the importance of mortality and the natural cycle of life and death. Tithonus's transformation from eager anticipation to regret serves as a cautionary tale, urging readers to appreciate the finite beauty of mortal existence rather than yearning for an unattainable eternity.

(iii) (a) Shane Koyczan's poem 'Beethoven' delves into the profound theme of love, using vivid imagery and emotional resonance. It discusses how Beethoven dealt with pain through his creativity. Beethoven, the iconic composer, suffered both physically and emotionally, unable to find love within the confines of his home. His father's abusive behaviour left scars that ran deep, making it challenging for him to connect with others. Therefore, he sought solace in his music—a refuge where he could express the inexpressible. Despite his deafness, he transformed emotion into symphonies creating a language that transcended mere notes. Koyczan's portrayal emphasises that, to truly understand Beethoven, one must listen to his compositions, for they reveal the depths of his soul and the universal power of love.

The statement 'Beethoven's pain and suffering translates into music, and music becomes his creative outlet' encapsulates the profound connection between the composer's emotional turmoil and his artistic expression. He grappled with other personal challenges too, such as hearing loss, unrequited love, and societal upheaval. His compositions, particularly during his middle and late periods, bear witness to this inner struggle. The Ninth Symphony, for instance, reflects both Beethoven's defiance in the face of adversity and his longing for universal brotherhood. The hauntingly beautiful 'Moonlight Sonata' resonates with melancholy, its delicate notes conveying a sense of introspection and vulnerability. Beethoven's ability to channel his suffering into music allowed him to transcend his own limitations and touch the hearts of generations. His compositions serve as a testament to the transformative power of art where pain finds solace and creativity becomes a beacon of hope.

(b) In John Donne's poem, 'Death Be Not Proud', the poet confronts Death challenging its power and arrogance. Instead of fearing death, the speaker challenges its power calling it 'not proud' and mocking its might. The poem suggests that death is not the end but a temporary state, akin to sleep.

Religious themes emerge, emphasising the idea of an afterlife and resurrection. By addressing Death directly, Donne's sonnet employs the literary device of apostrophe which allows the speaker to assert authority over this formidable adversary.

The confident tone of the poem provides an ironic sense of comfort to the readers by implicitly suggesting that Death is not to be feared at all. He further suggests that, in the end, Death will be overcome by something even greater. The closing lines proclaim that 'Death shall be no more' reinforcing the speaker's faith in eternal life beyond the mortal realm. The poet has also used Christian theology of eternity to taunt Death by telling him, 'Even if you take my physical body, you can never truly kill me.'

In conclusion, through 'Death Be Not Proud', the poet comes off as defiant and he invites readers to contemplate mortality, challenge fear and embrace the possibility of eternal life.

SQP Code : **PB-2/10**	Series ***i*-Succeed 2-25/10**	Roll No.

Sample Question Paper 02

Literature in English 12th (Code 801)

General Instructions

1. It has 5 questions in all.
2. Answer all questions.
3. While answering Question 1 in Section A, you are required to write only ONE option as the correct answer.
4. Internal choice has been given in the long answer questions on Drama, Prose and Poetry.
5. Do not exceed the prescribed word limit while answering the questions in Section B.
6. The intended marks for questions are given in brackets [ ].

Time : 3 Hrs.

Max. Marks : 80

Section A *(20 Marks)*

Question 1.

Choose the correct option for the following questions. (10)

(i) In the lines, 'Let this evil hour be marked forever in the calendar as cursed. You outside, come in!' from Act IV Scene 1, who is Macbeth calling? [Recall]

(a) The murderers
(b) The Servant
(c) Banquo
(d) Lennox

(ii) What song do the three Witches sing while dancing around the cauldron? [Recall]

(a) Prayers to Hecate
(b) Black spirits
(c) Thunderstorms
(d) Black night

(iii) What do you infer from the lines – 'Then the liars are fools, for there are enough liars in the world to beat up the honest men and hang them'- by Macduff's son from Act IV Scene 2? [Interpret]

(a) There are more liars than honest people
(b) It is better to be a liar than being an honest person
(c) Honest people must be punished
(d) Liars must be punished

(iv) According to Act V of *Macbeth*, which one of the following do you think is the cause of Lady Macbeth's sleepwalking? [Understanding]

(P) Macbeth's great ambitions
(Q) The Witches' prophecies
(R) The guilt of murdering Duncan
(S) The truth behind the murders

(a) (P) and (R)
(b) (R) and (S)
(c) (P) and (Q)
(d) (Q) and (S)

(v) Read the two statements from the short story 'There Will Come Soft Rains' and choose the correct option from the ones given below. [Analysis]

Statement I The entire West face of the house was black, save for five places.

Statement II ...and opposite him a girl, hands raised to catch a ball which never came down.

(a) Statement I and II are related.

(b) Statement I and II are not related to each other.

(c) Statement II is the reason for Statement I.

(d) Statement I is the reason for Statement II.

(vi) In the short story 'Atithi', Motilal Babu took in Tarapada as [Understanding]

(a) he wanted a son
(b) he needed a hand in business
(c) he was impressed by Tarapada
(d) Tarapada desperately needed shelter

(vii) In the story 'Indigo', who helped Aniruddha find food and shelter at the Dak Bungalow? [Recall]

(a) Promode
(b) Uncle Mohit
(c) Bhola Babu
(d) Sukhanram

(viii) What is the main idea of the poem 'Death Be Not Proud'? [Analysis]

(a) An argument against power of Death
(b) Death should be feared
(c) Death is inevitable
(d) An entity described as Death

(ix) Who is the speaker in the poem 'Tithonus'? [Recall]

(a) Goddess Aurora
(b) Tithonus
(c) The God of Sky
(d) The Sun God Apollo

(x) The meaning of 'dreadful silence' according to the poem 'Small Towns and the River' is [Interpret]

(a) the silence due to someone's death.
(b) the silence of peace.
(c) the eerie silence of small towns at curfew.
(d) None of these

Question 2.

SP-02

Complete the following sentences by providing a reason for each in brief. Do not write the question. (10)

(i) In the play, Macbeth wants Banquo and Fleance dead because .... [Understanding]

(ii) Lady Macbeth chides her husband because .... [Analysis]

(iii) In the beginning of Act III, Lady Macbeth and Macbeth organise a banquet because .... [Recall]

(iv) The Witches play an important role in the play *Macbeth* because .... [Understanding]

(v) In the short story 'Atithi', Tarapada had left his family because .... [Interpret]

(vi) In the short story 'The Medicine Bag', Martin said 'Hi' to Grandpa with his head down because .... [Analysis]

(vii) The house in the story 'There Will Come Soft Rains' was empty because .... [Recall]

(viii) In the poem 'Telephone Conversation', the speaker informs the Landlady that he is from Africa because .... [Recall]

(ix) Tithonus first views immortality as a blessing but later regrets it because .... [Analysis]

(x) The poet is not afraid of death in the poem 'Death Be Not Proud' because .... [Understanding]

Section B (60 Marks)

Macbeth-William Shakespeare

Question 3.

(i) What prophecy does Banquo recall at the end of the opening of Act III ? How does Macbeth react to the prophecy? Give your answer in 100-150 words. [Recall and Understanding] (5)

(a) Banquo's suspicions (b) Macbeth's fears

(ii) Describe the change in Lady Macbeth's behaviour. What does this reveal about Macbeth's moral state? Give your answer in 100-150 words. [Analysis] (5)

(a) Events that lead to the change

(b) The characteristic changes in Lady Macbeth noted by the doctor

(iii) (a) Comment on Macbeth's soliloquy in Act III, Scene 1, 'To be the king is nothing if I'm not safe as the king. I'm very afraid of Banquo…'. Give your answer in 200-250 words. [Evaluate] (10)

Or

(b) Discuss the conversation between Macduff's wife and son after he flees to England. What do you infer about their characters from this conversation? Give your answer in 200-250 words. [Understanding]

Prism-A Collection of Short Stories

Question 4.

(i) Examine the emotion of the speaker as he says 'I felt cold and hot at the same time as I recognised the man. 'Oh, no!' I whispered. 'It's Grandpa!' based on the story 'The Medicine Bag'. Incorporate the following details and give your answer in 100-150 words. [Evaluate] (5)

(a) The commotion in the street

(b) The feelings of the speaker as he goes inside the house

(ii) From the story 'There Will Come Soft Rains', discuss the literary devices used to highlight the theme of the story. Give your answer in 100-150 words, including the following points [Understanding] (5)

(a) The absence of humans (b) The fire element

(iii) (a) Describe Aniruddha's car journey based on the story 'Indigo' and evaluate how his circumstances led him to the Dak Bungalow in 200-250 words. [Analysis] (10)

Or

(b) Analyse the theme of the story 'The Cookie Lady'. What hidden message do you think the story has? And, how is it relevant in real life? Give your answer in 200-250 words. [Analysis]

SP-02

Rhapsody-Poetry

Question 5.

(i) What is the central idea of the poem 'Beethoven'? Give your answer in 100-150 words incorporating the following details. [Recall and Understanding] (5)

(a) The metaphor for the character's artistic struggle

(b) The use of vivid imagery in the poem

(ii) In the poem 'Small Towns and the River', why does the poet say 'The river has a soul...'. Incorporate the following details and write your answer in 100-150 words. [Analysis] (5)

(a) The river seeking a land of fish and stars

(b) Description of the speaker's hometown

(iii) (a) Evaluate Tithonus' reflections on the past. What does it say about the consequences of unchecked human desires? Give your answer in 200-250 words. [Evaluate] (10)

Or

(b) In the poem 'Telephone Conversation', what do the lines, 'I hate a wasted journey—I am African.' Silence. Silenced transmission of Pressurised good-breeding..." signify? Discuss the character of the landlady based on the conversation in the poem. Give your answer in 200-250 words. [Understanding]

Answers *in Topper's Style*

1. (i) (d) Lennox
(ii) (b) Black spirits
(iii) (a) There are more liars than honest people
(iv) (b) (R) and (S)
(v) (a) Statement I and II are related.
(vi) (c) he was impressed by Tarapada
(vii) (d) Sukhanram
(viii) (a) An argument against power of Death
(ix) (b) Tithonus
(x) (a) the silence due to someone's death.

2. (i) he fears the prophecy coming true and Banquo's sons acquiring the throne
(ii) she believes that Macbeth's hesitation and guilt are hindering their ambitious plans to seize the throne
(iii) they are celebrating Macbeth's coronation and his acquisition of the throne
(iv) their prophecies guide Macbeth's actions and push him towards darkness as he tries to fight his fate
(v) he had a deep urge to break free from bonds of all kinds, even the bonds of his family's affection
(vi) he felt ashamed and embarrassed as his Grandpa didn't fit the glamorous image of TV Indians
(vii) all the inhabitants had perished due to a nuclear blast
(viii) racial prejudice was prevalent in post-war Britain and people often refused to rent out their properties to those they regarded as racially inferior
(ix) reality strikes him and he keeps getting older, laden with physical limitations while his beloved Aurora remains youthful and beautiful
(x) according to the poet, it is not the ultimate act but merely a transition, a temporary rest, before eternal life

3. (i) In Act III of William Shakespeare's play *'Macbeth'*, Banquo recalls the prophecy made by the three witches. They foretold that Macbeth would become king and Banquo's descendants would eventually acquire the throne. Thus, Banquo becomes suspicious of Macbeth's rise to power and suspects that he has used unnatural means to ensure it. He further worries that the prophecy about his own lineage will also come true.

Macbeth, on the other hand, reacts with fear and paranoia to the prophecies regarding Banquo's sons leading the kingdom and inheriting the throne. To eliminate this threat to his power, Macbeth arranges for Banquo's murder, revealing his ruthless ambition and descent into darkness for fulfilling his desires to be the only man of power in the kingdom.

(ii) In William Shakespeare's tragedy *'Macbeth'*, Lady Macbeth undergoes a significant transformation throughout the play. Initially, she is ambitious, manipulative and she encourages her husband to commit regicide to seize the throne. However, as the play progresses, her guilt consumes her. The events that lead to this change include Duncan's murder, Banquo's ghost haunting Macbeth and the unravelling of their power-hungry plot. Lady Macbeth's sleepwalking scene reveals her tormented conscience. The doctor observes her walking around with a candle in her hand in the middle of the night, compulsively washing her hands saying fearful things out loud and talking to herself in circles. This is a symbolic attempt to cleanse herself of guilt. This shift in Lady Macbeth's behaviour highlights Macbeth's moral decline. His ruthless pursuit of power had not only corrupted him but also shattered his wife's sanity.

(iii) (a) In Act III, Scene 1 of the play, Macbeth delivers a soliloquy that reveals his inner turmoil and growing paranoia due to the circumstances he was facing. Macbeth had recently ascended to the throne, but his newfound kingship was overshadowed by fear and insecurity.

The soliloquy begins with the lines: 'To be thus is nothing; But to be safe thus.' Macbeth acknowledges that mere kingship holds little value if he cannot maintain his safety and security. His obsession with maintaining power consumes him and he fixates on the threat posed by Banquo.

Macbeth describes Banquo as possessing a 'royalty of nature' that makes him both courageous and wise. Banquo's lineage, as foretold by the witches, threatens Macbeth's position. According to the prophecy, Banquo's descendants are destined to become kings while Macbeth's own lineage remains uncertain. This uncertainty fuels Macbeth's fear and drives him to contemplate dark deeds.

The soliloquy reflects Macbeth's moral deterioration. His ambition has led him down a treacherous path, and now he grapples with the consequences. The juxtaposition of power and vulnerability highlights the tragedy of Macbeth's character. He is a king haunted by guilt willing to sacrifice anything, even friendship and honour, only just to secure his reign. Ultimately, this soliloquy foreshadows the violence and betrayal that will unfold as Macbeth seeks to eliminate the threat posed by Banquo and his lineage.

(b) In Act IV, Scene 2 of William Shakespeare's play *'Macbeth'*, there is a poignant exchange between Lady Macduff and her young son. Their conversation provides an insight into their characters. Lady Macduff is bewildered and hurt by her husband Macduff's sudden departure to England. She questions Ross demanding an explanation for his flight as she cannot comprehend why Macduff would leave his family vulnerable during such dangerous times.

Her concern for her child and her sense of betrayal are palpable. Thus, Lady Macduff represents innocence and vulnerability contrasting sharply with the ruthless ambition and cruelty that pervades the play.

Lady Macduff's son, though young, displays remarkable insight which can be easily inferred from the conversation he has with his mother after his father's departure. When Lady Macduff informs him that his father is dead, he astutely argues that he is not. His refusal to accept the news reflects his resilience and determination. He refuses to be deceived by appearances and clings to hope. Hence, the son's character embodies innocence, loyalty and a refusal to surrender to despair, even in dire circumstances.

At the end, Lady Macduff and her son are interrupted by a messenger who warns them of danger to their lives. However, they don't escape in time when the murderers enter, and, despite Lady Macduff's protests of innocence, they kill her son. Therefore, Lady Macduff's emotional turmoil and her son's perceptive resilience reveal the human cost of ambition and betrayal. Their characters serve as a stark contrast to the power-hungry and treacherous figures in the play, emphasising the tragedy that unfolds as Macbeth's reign spirals into chaos.

4. (i) In Virginia Driving Hawk Sneve's short story 'The Medicine Bag', the speaker experiences a tumultuous mix of emotions upon recognising the man walking down the street as his Grandpa. The street erupts with noise, a chorus of barking dogs and shouting children. A crowd of little kids surrounds someone, and the dogs yip and growl around this mysterious figure. When he goes closer to check, he recognises the man as his Grandpa.

Martin's initial shock turns into a whirlwind of sensations, simultaneous cold and heat. His whispered exclamation—'Oh, no! It's Grandpa!' reveals both surprise and anxiety. The unexpected visit threatens Martin's carefully constructed image of his grandfather which he shares with friends. His grandfather is not big and strong as Indians are usually portrayed by the media so he feels ashamed and embarrassed by his unannounced arrival. However, as he enters the house, conflicting emotions, embarrassment, curiosity and perhaps even affection swirl within him. This happens because no matter what his friends might think, he still loves his Grandpa.

(ii) In Ray Bradbury's science fiction short story 'There Will Come Soft Rains', several literary devices highlight the theme of humanity's insignificance in the face of technological advancement and destruction. The story lacks any living human characters which emphasises their absence.

The house, which is an automated relic, becomes the central character continuing its routines despite the vanished inhabitants. This absence highlights the eerie emptiness and the irreversible impact of an atomic catastrophe.

The 'radioactive glow' in the story implies that the town has suffered an atomic bomb attack.The house's west wall bears black burn marks with shadows of its former residents etched there. The fire element symbolises both destruction and endurance and the house stands as a testament to human ingenuity even after its occupants have perished.

(iii) (a) Aniruddha Bose sets off on a tragic car ride that takes unexpected turns and finally brings him to the unsettling Dak Bungalow in Satyajit Ray's short story 'Indigo'. Twenty-nine-year-old Aniruddha, a bachelor employed at an advertising agency, makes the decision to pay his friend Promode a visit in Dumka. His journey had a few small setbacks at the beginning including a flat tyre at the military barracks in Panagarh and queries from neighbours. Unfazed, he goes on to describe the cities and the unclouded blue sky. But once more, fate steps in, causing another tyre to rupture during a thunderstorm. Aniruddha discovers that he has made a mistake and is at a dead end when it is becoming dark and he has no spare tyres. In desperation, he sees what appears to be a window in the distance.

Pulling out his torch, he finds an old man named Sukhanram who offers him shelter in the Dak Bungalow. Aniruddha learns that the bungalow once belonged to an English sahib who was an indigo planter. The nearby factory's chimney stands as a lonely relic. That night, strange occurrences unfold: scratching at the door, a missing wristwatch and a vanished suitcase. Aniruddha's hands turn pale, his voice becomes English and his clothes change. He feels possessed by the spirit of the greedy planter and experiences a chilling transformation. Ultimately, Aniruddha's car journey takes him on a supernatural adventure with interesting twists and turns.

(b) Philip K. Dick's short story 'The Cookie Lady' explores various themes including loneliness, ignorance and exploitation. The story revolves around a dysfunctional and exploitative relationship with neither of the protagonists showing genuine interest in the other. Bubber only visits the old lady, Mrs. Drew, to feed his cookie cravings but Mrs. Drew has more sinister ambitions wishing to take Bubber's youth and strength.

In the story, Mrs. Drew is shown as a lonely old lady who lives in a dilapidated old house in Bubber's neighbourhood. She has no one to talk to and people ignore her due to her peculiar appearance and demeanour. That's why she becomes desperate to have Bubber visit her and tries to lure him into her house. By baking the cookies, Mrs. Drew succeeds in inviting Bubber into her home, and continues to do so as his presence has a magical effect on her and turns her into a beautiful young woman. In this scenario, she plays the part of a witch who ruthlessly exploits anyone she comes in contact with. As a vampire drains blood from innocent people, this evil lady sucks the youth and vitality of an overweight, obsessive child. In today's world, the relevance to this story can be seen almost everywhere where kind and innocent people are usually taken advantage of by those in powerful positions.

The story also emphasises the obligation of parents to guide their children. His parents' lack of concern causes Bubber to fall into the trap of an unscrupulous lady who, under the guise of giving him with cookies, exploits his youth and drains his vitality turning him into dry weed carried by the winds.

5. (i) The central idea of the poem 'Beethoven' revolves around the indomitable spirit of artistic creation and the triumph of the human will over adversity. The poet begins and ends the poem with the word 'Listen' emphasising that understanding Beethoven lies in experiencing his music. Despite Beethoven's deafness, he continues to compose beautiful music in his mind. The metaphor for his artistic struggle lies in the juxtaposition of his physical limitations with the boundless realm of imagination where music becomes his creative outlet. His father's constant dissatisfaction, 'Not good enough', echoes the external pressures that all artists face. Yet, Beethoven's inner world remains vivid and alive transcending his silent ears. The poem celebrates the resilience of the creative spirit urging us to 'listen' beyond the surface and recognise the enduring power of Beethoven's compositions.

(ii) In Mamang Dai's poem 'Small Towns and the River', the line 'The river has a soul' carries profound symbolism. The river, personified, yearns for something more than its current existence. The desire to discover a 'land of fish and stars' implies a mythical, otherworldly realm that is an escape from everyday life. The river's soul pursues transcendence echoing human yearnings for something more.

The speaker describes their hometown as a peaceful place tucked among the forest of trees. The town remains unchanged regardless of the seasons or events.

This unwavering stability contrasts with the river's unending flow. The river's immortality contrasts sharply with the mortal nature of human life in small towns. Therefore, in essence, the river symbolises continuity, longing, the eternal quest for meaning and a poignant reflection on life's impermanence and the soul's yearning for something beyond earthly confines.

(iii) (a) In Alfred, Lord Tennyson's poem 'Tithonus', the speaker Tithonus reflects on the tragic consequences of unchecked human desires. The mythological figure Tithonus, a prince of Troy, fell in love with Aurora, the goddess of dawn. Desiring eternal companionship, Tithonus begged Aurora to grant him immortality. She complied but her oversight led to his suffering. Though she grants him immortality, she misses to add eternal youthfulness to the wishes. Tithonus ages relentlessly becoming unspeakably ancient and longs for the ordinary fate of mortality—a desire he once rejected. The poem serves as a cautionary tale urging us to consider the consequences of our desires and appreciate the natural order of life. It reminds us that some desires, when fulfilled without wisdom, can transform our blessings into our greatest burdens.

Tithonus' plea for immortality reveals the human tendency to desire more than what is natural or necessary. Aurora's granting of his wish parallels how wealthy individuals often give without considering the consequences of it. On the other hand, Tithonus's unchecked desire for immortality leads him to an eternal suffering. The 'strong Hours' (personified as fate or destiny) work their will leaving him maimed and trapped in a twilight existence. He dwells alongside immortal youth but remains a shadow of his former self, consumed by the curse.

(b) In Wole Soyinka's poem 'Telephone Conversation', the lines 'I hate a wasted journey—I am African.' Silence. Silenced transmission of Pressurised good-breeding" carry significant meaning and reveal the character of the landlady. The speaker, who is an African man, seeks to rent an apartment in Britain. Initially, the white landlady is pleasant but her attitude changes when she learns he is African.

The silence that follows his confession reflects her shock and prejudice which was prevalent at the time. She is taken aback by his ethnicity and her silence clearly reveals her discomfort. The phrase 'pressurised good-breeding' suggests that the landlady adheres to social norms and politeness. Despite her prejudice, she maintains decorum suppressing any overt expression of racism. Thus, her silence is a result of this internal struggle.

Racial bigotry is exemplified by the landlady's actions. Her limited perspective is exposed as she assesses the speaker based only on the colour of his skin. Her obsession with racial stereotypes is further shown by her being intent on finding out about his lightness or darkness. By comparing the speaker's clever reaction with the ridiculousness of such discrimination, the poet skillfully highlights its absurdity. In conclusion, the landlady is shown in the poem as being both polite and prejudiced. The speaker's astute remark and her silence highlight the detrimental effects of racial prejudice. Through this brief phone conversation, Soyinka brilliantly exposes the intricacies of human interaction and the persuasive power of language while critically condemning racism.

SQP Code : **PB-3/10** Series ***i*-Succeed 3-25/10** Roll No.

Sample Question Paper 03

Literature in English 12th (Code 801)

General Instructions

1. It has 5 questions in all.
2. Answer all questions.
3. While answering Question 1 in Section A, you are required to write only ONE option as the correct answer.
4. Internal choice has been given in the long answer questions on Drama, Prose and Poetry.
5. Do not exceed the prescribed word limit while answering the questions in Section B.
6. The intended marks for questions are given in brackets [ ].

Time : 3 Hrs.

Max. Marks : 80

Section A *(20 Marks)*

Question 1.

Choose the correct option for the following questions. (10)

(i) What are the names of King Duncan's sons in the play *Macbeth*? [Recall]

(a) Lennox and Macduff (b) Siward and Edward
(c) Ross and Fleance (d) Malcolm and Donalbain

(ii) In Act V, how do the soldiers conceal themselves before attacking Macbeth's castle? [Interpret]

(a) They hide in the castle (b) They hide in the Birnam forest
(c) They hide behind boulders (d) They hide at the river bank

(iii) Who informs Macbeth of Lady Macbeth's death in Act V of the play? [Recall]

(a) Lennox (b) Siward
(c) Malcolm (d) Seyton

(iv) According to Act III of *Macbeth*, why is Hecate angry? [Analysis]

(P)The witches gave the prophecies to Macbeth
(Q) The witches did not ask for Hecate's permission
(R) The witches did not present their offerings to Hecate
(S) The witches made a mistake while preparing charms

(a) (P) and (Q) (b) (Q) and (R)
(c) (R) and (S) (d) (P) and (S)

(v) Read the two statements from the short story 'Indigo' and choose the correct option from the ones given below. [Analysis]

Statements I Is there a place here where I can stay the night?

Statements II But that's a long way. Shouldn't you have arranged for a driver?

(a) Statement I and II are similar.
(b) Statement I and II are not related to each other.
(c) Statement II is the reason for Statement I.
(d) Statement I is the reason for Statement II.

(vi) In the story 'There Will Come Soft Rains', which dish's aroma lures the dog into the house? [Recall]

(a) Brownies
(b) Toast
(c) Pancakes
(d) Cookies

(vii) Mrs. Drew experiences changes when Bubber visits her. What are those changes? [Understanding]

(a) She is reminded of her childhood
(b) She feels loved and cared for
(c) She gets rejuvenated and supernaturally becomes younger
(d) She feels sad and contemplates her future

(viii) How are 'madness' and 'genius' described in the poem 'Beethoven'? [Understanding]

(a) Inseparable
(b) Unique
(c) Conflicting
(d) Mutually exclusive

(ix) In the poem 'Tithonus', themes that are prominent are [Interpret]

(a) human wishes and unquenched desires.
(b) love and war.
(c) immortality and time.
(d) beauty and wrath of nature.

(x) In what way does the river resemble human life, in the poem 'Small Towns and the River'? [Interpret]

(a) In its constant flow
(b) In its fragility
(c) In its permanence
(d) In its transience

Question 2.

Complete the following sentences by providing a reason for each in brief. Do not write the question. (10)

SP-03

(i) In Act III, Macbeth tells Lady Macbeth that he would visit the three Witches again because .... [Recall]

(ii) In Act III Scene 4, Macbeth says in the court that all the seats are occupied because .... [Recall]

(iii) In Act IV Scene 3, Lady Macduff says, "Fathered he is, and yet he's fatherless" because .... [Understanding]

(iv) In Act V, Lady Macbeth in her sleep constantly washes her hand because .... [Analysis]

(v) In the story 'There Will Come Soft Rains', there are charcoal stains on the outer walls of the house because .... [Understanding]

(vi) In the short story 'Atithi', Tarapada wanted to go to Nandigram because .... [Recall]

(vii) In the short story 'Indigo', Aniruddha considered himself an expert on the topic of indigo plantations because .... [Understanding]

(viii) In the poem 'Beethoven', he tries to 'feel the vibrations' of the music because .... [Understanding]

(ix) In the poem 'Small Towns and the River', the poet calls the silence dreadful because .... [Analysis]

(x) In the poem 'Death Be not Proud', Death is portrayed as a servant to fate and chance because .... [Understanding]

Section B *(60 Marks)*

Macbeth-William Shakespeare

Question 3.

(i) In Act III, Macbeth says, 'The worm that's fled Hath nature that in time will venom breed, No teeth for the present'. What does he mean by these lines? Give your answer in 100-150 words including the following points: [Understanding] (5)

(a) Macbeth's soliloquy (b) Macbeth feels varied emotions

(ii) In Act III, Scene 4, what do you infer from Lady Macbeth's words, "Oh, that's nonsense! This is just another one of the hallucinations you always get when you're afraid...". Give your answer in 100-150 words incorporating the following details: [Interpret] (5)

(a) Who is Lady Macbeth talking to in the given lines?

(b) The things that she is trying to conceal

(iii) (a) What do you infer about Macbeth's character from his reaction to Lady Macbeth's death in Act V? Discuss their relationship in the acts studied and give your answer in 200-250 words. [Evaluate] (10)

Or

(b) Macbeth sealed his doom by believing the Witches' prophecies and acting on them in order to control his future. Comment on how his greed led him to his destruction and answer the question in 200-250 words. [Analysis]

Prism-A Collection of Short Stories

Question 4.

SP-03

(i) In the story 'The Cookie Lady', why didn't Bubber notice the changes in Mrs. Drew? Answer the question in 100-150 words incorporating the following details. [Understanding] (5)

(a) Changes in Mrs. Drew's appearance

(b) Bubber's repeatedly visiting Mrs. Drew

(ii) Describe Grandpa's character based on the story 'The Medicine Bag'. Incorporating the following details, provide the answer in 100-150 words. [Interpret] (5)

(a) The importance of Grandpa's Medicine Bag

(b) Grandpa's appearance

(iii) (a) Tarapada did not stay at one place for a long time but he spent almost two years at Motilal Babu's home. Based on the short story 'Atithi', evaluate the given statement in 200-250 words. [Evaluate] (10)

Or

(b) Comment on the relevance of the title 'There Will Come Soft Rains' for the prescribed story. Give your answer in 200-250 words. [Analysis]

Rhapsody-Poetry

Question 5.

(i) In the poem 'Death Be Not Proud', what do you infer from the lines- 'From rest and sleep, which but thy pictures be, Much pleasure; then from thee much more must flow'? Give your answer in 100-150 words incorporating the following details: [Interpret] (5)

(a) Poet's feelings about 'death'

(b) The literary device(s) used in the given lines

(ii) State the relevance of the line 'The woods decay, the woods decay and fall' in the poem 'Tithonus'. Give your answer in 100-150 words incorporating the following details: [Evaluate] (5)

(a) Who is the speaker here?

(b) The speaker relating to the natural world.

(iii) (a) In the poem 'Small Towns and the River', discuss the linguistic devices employed by the poet to deliver the desire of the people in small towns to 'walk with the gods'. Write the answer in 200-250 words. [Analysis] (10)

Or

(b) Based on the poem 'Telephone Conversation', discuss why the landlady mentions she lives 'off premises' and what effect does it have on the power dynamic of the conversation? Give your answer in 200-250 words. [Analysis]

Answers *in Topper's Style*

1. (i) (d) Malcolm and Donalbain
(ii) (b) They hide in the Birnam forest
(iii) (d) Seyton
(iv) (a) (P) and (Q)
(v) (b) Statement I and II are not related to each other.
(vi) (c) Pancakes
(vii) (c) She gets rejuvenated and supernaturally becomes younger
(viii) (a) Inseparable
(ix) (c) immortality and time.
(x) (a) In its constant flow

2. (i) he was anxious regarding maintaining his position as a king and wanted to know more about his future to prepare for it
(ii) he sees Banquo's ghost seated in the chair reserved for him at the court
(iii) Macduff flees and leaves her and their child without any protection
(iv) she sees blood on her hands as evidence of her and Macbeth's crimes
(v) the house stands as a lone survivor in a desolate California city after a nuclear catastrophe
(vi) the landlord there was setting up a new theatre company which he thought of joining
(vii) for the past few months, he had not been writing and had spent most of his time reading about the indigo plantations in Bengal and Bihar regions
(viii) he is deaf and can't hear the music his piano produces
(ix) it echoes loss, mortality and impermanence of human life while the river flows inexorably, indifferent to time and death
(x) it does not have any authority and lacks autonomy

3. (i) In these lines from Act III, Scene 4 of the play, Macbeth speaks to himself contemplating the escape of Fleance Banquo' son. The 'worm' refers to Fleance who is young and harmless now ('no teeth for the present') but is prophesied by the three witches to father a line of kings. Macbeth fears that Fleance will grow to be a threat (venom breed) to his own power in time. His words reveal his deep anxiety and paranoia as he recognises the potential danger in leaving any threat to his throne alive. This moment emphasises Macbeth's descent into tyranny as he

becomes increasingly consumed by the need to secure his ill-gotten crown.

(ii) In Act III, Scene 4 of the play, Lady Macbeth addresses her husband, Macbeth, with these words in an attempt to dismiss his visible agitation upon seeing the ghost of Banquo at the royal banquet. She attempts to conceal the reality of Macbeth's guilt-induced hallucinations from the assembled guests as she wishes to maintain their royal facade and prevent any suspicion regarding their involvement in Banquo's murder. She is afraid that Macbeth's disturbing reactions to his own mind's manifestation (Banquo's ghost) may reveal the truth. Her words serve as a desperate effort to uphold the semblance of stability and rationality in the face of Macbeth's unravelling psyche reflecting her own deep-seated denial and complicity in their shared crimes.

(iii) (a) Macbeth's reaction to Lady Macbeth's death in Act V reveals crucial aspects of his character while their relationship undergoes significant shifts throughout the play. When Macbeth receives news of his wife's sudden demise, he responds with a mixture of indifference and resignation. Deserted by his followers and awaiting the enemy's attack, he even contemplates suicide. However, the shock of the messenger's report snaps him back to reality. This reaction highlights Macbeth's emotional detachment and the toll that guilt and ambition have taken on his psyche.

Macbeth and Lady Macbeth's relationship evolves from being 'partners in greatness' to a complex dynamic marked by manipulation and ambition. Initially, Macbeth trusts Lady Macbeth and values her advice in important matters of his life. She, too, eagerly supports his ascent to power urging him to seize the throne as per the prophecies. Lady Macbeth's strength lies in her ability to manipulate Macbeth effectively pushing him toward regicide. She chastises his hesitation questioning his manhood until he decides to kill King Duncan. However, as Macbeth becomes the king, he distances himself from her influence. He secretly plans Banquo's murder without consulting her revealing a growing self-reliance. On the other hand, Lady Macbeth, who was once resolute, descends into madness due to her guilt. Her sleepwalking scenes symbolise her inner torment and she ultimately dies under this torment. Their partnership-in-crime unravels through the course of the play leaving Macbeth isolated and haunted by their deeds.

Therefore, to summarise, Macbeth's reaction to Lady Macbeth's death underscores his emotional numbness, apathy and blinding ambition while their relationship shifts from collaboration to tragedy reflecting the destructive consequences of unchecked ambition and guilt.

(b) Macbeth's tragic downfall in the play *'Macbeth'* is intricately tied to his insatiable greed and his willingness to act upon the Witches' prophecies. When the Witches hail Macbeth as the Thane of Glamis, Thane of Cawdor, and future king, they ignite his ambition and the tantalising prospect of power consumes him completely in that moment.

Macbeth's initial scepticism gives way to curiosity and he becomes obsessed with the concept of fulfilling the prophecies. His desire for power makes him blind to the repercussions of his actions. Macbeth murders King Duncan, motivated by Lady Macbeth's persuasion and personal desires. His desire for the throne outweighs all moral considerations. This behaviour sets a perilous precedent. Macbeth's desire for power grows driving him to kill anybody who stands in his way including Banquo, Macduff's family and others. As his anxiety rises and consumes him, he eventually fears losing the throne. He orders Banquo's death to prevent the Witches' prophecy regarding Banquo's descendants. His desire for security drives him into committing further inhumane acts driving Scotland into a state of chaos. Macbeth's guilt and paranoia plague him. He experiences hallucinations including seeing Banquo's ghost and hearing voices. His desire for dominance evolved into an unquenchable appetite for survival. He seeks reassurance from the Witches, thereby sealing his doom.

Macbeth's greed blinds him to the certainty of his own demise. He thinks he's invincible because of the Witches' predictions. In the last battle, Macduff reveals that he was "from his mother's womb untimely ripped" contradicting the Witches' prediction and Macbeth realises his greed had deceived him.

4. (i) In the story 'The Cookie Lady', Mrs. Drew's transformation remains unnoticed by Bubber due to her cunning manipulation and his youthful innocence. Bubber's sole motivation to visit her was the cookies that he would get to eat, due to which he failed to notice what was happening in his surroundings.

Initially, Mrs. Drew appears as an elderly woman, known as the creepy old lady in the neighbourhood due to her scary appearance and weird behaviour. Bubber visited her regularly, drawn by her freshly baked cookies which were his favourite treat. Knowing his weakness, Mrs. Drew had lured him into her house and as he devoured the cookies and read to her from his school books, she intently watched him. In a strange twist, she began to rejuvenate, her withered skin plumping up and wrinkles disappearing whenever she would sit close to Bubber. However, this transformation is temporary and she reverts to her old self once Bubber leaves.

(ii) In the short story 'The Medicine Bag', Grandpa's character is multifaceted reflecting both cultural significance and personal wisdom. His 'medicine bag', a cherished heirloom, symbolises his heritage and spiritual connection. The bag contains sacred objects, including eagle feathers and a buffalo horn spoon, which he uses for rituals and guidance.

Grandpa's appearance is described as weathered, with deeply lined features and a stooped posture. His eyes, however, hold a timeless wisdom revealing a profound understanding of life. Despite his frailty, Grandpa exudes strength and resilience embodying the resilience of his people. His role extends beyond the physical and he serves as a bridge between generations imparting ancestral knowledge to his grandson, Martin. Grandpa's quiet demeanour conceals a wealth of cultural richness emphasising the importance of heritage and the continuity of tradition. His character exemplifies the delicate balance between past and present, and his Medicine Bag becomes a tangible link to his ancestral wisdom.

(iii) (a) In the short story 'Atithi' by Rabindranath Tagore, the statement that Tarapada did not stay at one place for long except for his extended stay at Motilal Babu's home holds significant thematic implications. Tarapada, a wandering ascetic, represents the transient nature of life and the impermanence of human connections. His nomadic lifestyle contrasts sharply with the settled existence of Motilal Babu and his family. Tarapada's arrival disrupts the routine of the household introducing an element of unpredictability and spiritual inquiry.

During his two-year stay, Tarapada becomes an integral part of the family and the village sharing meals, stories, helping people around, learning new things and having philosophical discussions. His presence challenges societal norms and materialistic pursuits emphasising the value of spiritual seeking over material possessions. From the members of Motilal Babu's family, to the people of the village, everyone feels touched and in awe of having met Tarapada. Through Tarapada, Tagore explores themes of hospitality, compassion and the search for deeper meaning in life's experiences. Despite his eventual departure, Tarapada leaves an indelible mark on Motilal Babu's family prompting introspection and a reevaluation of their priorities in life. Thus, the statement underscores the transformative power of unexpected encounters and the enduring impact of transient guests in our lives.

(b) The title 'There Will Come Soft Rains' holds profound significance in Ray Bradbury's short story. Derived from Sara Teasdale's poem, which Bradbury references, the title encapsulates the central theme of the narrative. Teasdale's poem, published in 1918, reflects on the aftermath of human extinction due to war, envisioning a world where nature continues its cycles despite humanity's absence. In Bradbury's story, set in a post-apocalyptic future, a mechanised house persists long after its inhabitants have perished in a nuclear catastrophe. The title alludes to the gentle, inevitable return of natural processes like soft rains, blooming flowers and the passage of time despite humanity's destructive tendencies. The house, devoid of life, mechanically performs its daily routines cooking meals, cleaning, reading out birthday/anniversary reminders and maintaining itself. Yet, its mechanical precision contrasts starkly with the absent human touch in the story emphasising the eerie emptiness.

The title serves as a poignant reminder of humanity's impermanence and the resilience of nature. It sheds light on the irony that while technology endures, the very beings it once served have vanished. This cautionary tale warns against unchecked technological advancement and the potential consequences of human hubris. Hence, the title encapsulates both the haunting beauty of nature's continuity and the tragic absence of human connection throughout the story.

5. (i) In John Donne's poem 'Death Be Not Proud', the poet challenges the conventional perception of death. The given lines "From rest and sleep, which but thy pictures be, Much pleasure; then from thee much more must flow" convey two significant aspects.

First, Donne's feelings about 'death' are paradoxical. He personifies death as a proud entity defying its supposed power. The poet suggests that death is merely a transition and a temporary state akin to rest or sleep. The imagery of 'pictures' implies that death is a mere reflection or shadow of existence. Donne views death as an intermediary stage before something greater unfolds.

Second, the literary device employed here is a paradox. By replacing 'rest and sleep' with 'much pleasure' and emphasising that 'much more must flow' from death, the poet subverts the traditional fear associated with dying. He implies that death leads to an even more profound experience, perhaps eternal life or even spiritual awakening.

The paradox highlights the poem's central theme which states the triumph of the soul over mortality. Through this clever wordplay, the poet invites readers to reconsider their perceptions of death and embrace the possibility of transcending it.

(ii) In the poem 'Tithonus', the line 'The woods decay, the woods decay and fall' holds profound thematic significance. Tithonus, the speaker, is a mortal who was granted immortality by the goddess Aurora (Eos). However, this gift soon becomes a curse for Tithonus. Unlike the natural world which ages, decays and eventually renews itself, Tithonus remains frozen in perpetual existence. The repetition of 'decay' in the poem shows the relentless passage of time for everything around, except him. He yearns for release longing to return to the earth's natural cycle of life and death. Tithonus' relationship with nature is one of envy and sorrow as he witnesses the beauty of renewal in the woods and the swan yet he himself is denied this natural rhythm. His immortality becomes a burden and a curse and he laments his inability to share in the organic processes that define human existence.

(iii) (a) There are multiple linguistic devices employed by Mamang Dai in her poem 'Small Towns and the River' in an attempt to convey the yearning of people in small towns to 'walk with the gods'.

The poem begins paradoxically as small towns typically evoke associations with themes like mortality and impermanence. However, here, the poet places the idea of death in contrast with the desire for divine connection. The very setting that symbolises loss becomes a place where souls aspire for transcendence.

The 'sad wreath of tuberoses' reflects not only grief but also the cyclical nature of life. Tuberoses, which are often associated with funerals, become a symbol of both mourning and renewal just like the river's eternal flow.

Throughout the poem, the lines flow seamlessly into one another as if mirroring the river's perpetual movement in every season and every moment. This enjambment highlights its contrast with the transient lives of the people of the town. The river itself embodies eternity persisting despite human mortality. Unlike the townspeople, it carries memories, hopes and perhaps divine guidance. The desire to "walk with the gods" becomes a metaphor for transcending earthly limitations. Poet's vivid imagery, personification and metaphors focusing on the river invite readers to contemplate the paradoxical relationship between permanence and impermanence, mortality and eternity.

(b) In the poem 'Telephone Conversation', the landlady's mention that she lives 'off premises' serves as a subtle yet powerful indicator of racial bias.

The landlady initially appears pleasant but her demeanour changes abruptly when the speaker reveals he is African. Although she had advertised the room without racial restrictions, her true feelings emerge soon. By emphasising that she lives 'off premises,' she implies that her personal space remains separate from the property she rents out. This distinction suggests hidden prejudice in which she doesn't want to share her immediate living environment with someone of a different race. The power dynamic becomes evident when her assertion of living 'off premises' establishes an imbalance. She holds the upper hand in this transaction. Her refusal to engage directly with the speaker's racial identity reinforces her authority. The silence that follows his confession further shows her control over the conversation. Meanwhile, the speaker's plea—"I hate a wasted journey"—reveals his vulnerability. He desperately seeks acceptance but the landlady's discriminatory stance leaves him at her mercy.

Throughout the poem, the poet masterfully employs irony and satire. The mundane act of seeking accommodation becomes an example of societal prejudice. The landlady's hypocrisy, publicly claiming non- discrimination while privately revealing her bias, exposes the absurdity of racial discrimination. The telephone, a symbol of communication, becomes a conduit for both connection and division here. With each word exchanged, the power dynamic shifts leaving the reader to contemplate the complexities of racial bias even in seemingly mundane interactions.

SQP Code : **PB-4/10** Series ***i*-Succeed 4-25/10** Roll No. | | | | | | | | |

Sample Question Paper 04

Literature in English 12th (Code 801)

General Instructions

1. It has 5 questions in all.
2. Answer all questions.
3. While answering Question 1 in Section A, you are required to write only ONE option as the correct answer.
4. Internal choice has been given in the long answer questions on Drama, Prose and Poetry.
5. Do not exceed the prescribed word limit while answering the questions in Section B.
6. The intended marks for questions are given in brackets [ ].

Time : 3 Hrs.

Max. Marks : 80

Section A (20 Marks)

Question 1.

Choose the correct option for the following questions. (10)

(i) Who is the speaker of the following lines according to Act III of the play *Macbeth*? [Recall]

'…And so, I pray, be you. Let your remembrance Apply to Banquo; present him eminence…'

(a) Banquo (b) The witches

(c) Lady Macbeth (d) Macbeth

(ii) In Act IV, Macbeth gets to hear witches' apparitions. Who is the first apparition about? [Recall]

(a) Banquo's sons (b) Macbeth's coronation

(c) Thane of Cawdor (d) Thane of Fife

(iii) Who is being referred to in the following line from Act V of *Macbeth*? 'Let them fly all.' [Recall]

(a) Thanes (b) Commoners

(c) Servants (d) Soldiers

(iv) Based on your reading of Acts III, IV and V, which of the following statements from the play reflects the character of Macbeth's soldiers? [Understanding]

(P) They are brave and highly motivated (Q) They are indifferent

(R) They lack loyalty and just follow orders (S) They are disloyal and unreliable

(a) (P) and (Q) (b) (Q) and (R)

(c) (R) and (S) (d) (S) and (Q)

(v) Read the two statements from the short story 'Atithi' and choose the correct option from the ones given below. [Analysis]

Statement I Charushashi was jealous of Sonamani because of Tarapada.

Statement II She did not like her parents praising him.

(a) Statement I and II are similar.

(b) Statement I and II are not related to each other.

(c) Statement II is the reason for Statement I.

(d) Statement I is the reason for Statement II.

(vi) In the story 'The Cookie Lady', Bubber randomly opened the blue book and the chapter was on [Recall]

(a) France (b) Brazil (c) Peru (d) Spain

(vii) How would you describe the mechanised house's response to the death of the dog in the story 'There Will Come Soft Rains'? [Understanding]

(a) Cruel and disturbing (b) Adaptive and advanced

(c) Kind and harmonious (d) Apt and distinct

(viii) What is the central idea of the poem 'Telephone Conversation'? [Interpret]

(a) Communication skills (b) Racial discrimination

(c) The colour prejudice (d) All of these

(ix) What do we learn from Beethoven in the poem? [Understanding]

(a) Pain and suffering are important (b) Hardships are part of life

(c) Resilience and Perseverance (d) Beauty in pain

(x) According to the poem 'Tithonus', what is something that the Gods cannot do? [Recall]

(a) Grant eternal youthfulness (b) Grant forgiveness

(c) Recall their gifts (d) Recall their words

Question 2.

Complete the following sentences by providing a reason for each in brief. Do not write the question. (10)

SP-04

(i) Macbeth is initially hesitant to fight Macduff, in Act V of the play *Macbeth* because .... [Understanding]

(ii) Lady Macbeth is filled with sorrow in the beginning of Act III because .... [Understanding]

(iii) The witches in the play *Macbeth* were able to control Macbeth because .... [Analysis]

(iv) In Act IV of the play, when Macduff flees, Ross defends him and stops Lady Macduff from saying cruel things about him because .... [Understanding]

(v) In the story 'Atithi', Tarapada learnt some songs and, just like a caged bird, flew away one morning because .... [Analysis]

(vi) In the story 'The Cookie Lady', Mrs. Drew wanted to touch Bubber's arm because .... [Recall]

(vii) In the story 'The Medicine Bag', Grandpa's scuffed old cowboy boots were tight because .... [Recall]

(viii) In the poem 'Telephone Conversation', 'sarcasm' has played an important role because .... [Interpret]

(ix) In the poem 'Tithonus', he says "Release me, and restore me to the ground" because .... [Analysis]

(x) The deaf has been described as having an intimacy with silence in the poem 'Beethoven' because .... [Analysis]

Section B *(60 Marks)*

Macbeth-William Shakespeare

Question 3.

(i) Who plans Banquo's death and what is the 'treachery' he talks about before dying in Act III? Give your answer in 100-150 words incorporating the following details. [Recall] (5)

(a) The identity of Banquo's killer

(b) The motivation of the killer

(ii) Give a description of the Witches' act in Act IV including the following details, in not more than 100-150 words. [Understanding] (5)

(a) The significance of the Witches' character

(b) The atmosphere of the play

(iii) (a) Discuss how Act IV becomes an important link between what is going on under Macbeth's rule versus what will happen as the play progresses. Write your answer in 200-250 words. [Evaluate] (10)

Or

(b) What do you infer about Macbeth's character in the play, from the conversation between Caithness and Angus? Comment in 200-250 words. [Interpret]

Prism-A Collection of Short Stories

Question 4.

(i) What was the effect of his travels on Tarapada in the story 'Atithi'? Give your answer in 100-150 words incorporating the following details. [Understanding] (5)

(a) The travels shaping Tarapada's character.

(b) The skills Tarapada learn

(ii) Describe what happened to Aniruddha when he suddenly woke up in Dak Bungalow in the middle of the night. Incorporate the following details and give your answer in 100-150 words based on your reading of the story 'Indigo'. [Evaluate] (5)

(a) Changes in his appearance (b) Changes in his surroundings

(iii) (a) Discuss the ending of the story 'The Cookie Lady'. Do you think it could have had a different end? Give your answer in 200-250 words based on your understanding of the story. [Analysis] (10)

Or

(b) Who do you think is the main character of the story 'There Will Come Soft Rains'? Give evidence for your answer in 200-250 words. [Recall and Evaluate]

Rhapsody-Poetry

Question 5.

(i) Discuss the linguistic devices employed by John Donne in his poem 'Death Be Not Proud' to highlight the impotence of death. Including the following details, answer the question in 100-150 words. [Evaluate] (5)

(a) The speaker is not afraid of death

(b) The impact of the end of the poem

(ii) Based on your reading of the poem 'Small Towns and The River', comment on the collective consciousness of the people of small towns in 100-150 words. Incorporate the following details in your answer. [Analysis] (5)

(a) The meaning of the line "Small towns growing with anxiety for the future"

(b) Theme of the poem

(iii) (a) From Alfred Tennyson's poem 'Tithonus', what lesson can we all learn as a society? Discuss in 200-250 words. [Understanding] (10)

Or

(b) Comment on society's unattainable beauty standards and discuss the impact of racial prejudice on people as per the prescribed poem 'Telephone Conversation'. [Interpret]

Answers *in Topper's Style*

1. (i) (d) Macbeth
(ii) (d) Thane of Fife
(iii) (a) Thanes
(iv) (b) Q and R
(v) (a) Statement I and II are similar.
(vi) (c) Peru
(vii) (a) Cruel and disturbing
(viii) (d) All of these
(ix) (c) Resilience and Perseverance
(x) (c) recall their gifts

2. (i) Macbeth had murdered Macduff's entire family and this guilt weighs heavily on him
(ii) she is worried that someone may find out the real cause of Duncan's death which is Macbeth and herself
(iii) he was already a corrupt man with high ambitions
(iv) he believes Macduff is a noble, judicious and wise person who must have left knowing it was necessary
(v) the teacher had started treating him like his own son
(vi) she wished to be rejuvenated with the feeling of youth again and couldn't resist the urge to supernaturally become young again
(vii) he had filled each one of them with money
(viii) it helped the speaker deal cleverly with the landlady's racial prejudice against him
(ix) he is overwhelmed by the burdensome consequences of immortality
(x) it is ever present in their dreams and it accentuates their relationship of quietude as they experience it

3. (i) In the play, it is Macbeth himself who orchestrates Banquo's murder. The witches' prophecy that Banquo's descendants will inherit the throne drives Macbeth to this step. He fears that Banquo has the potential to challenge his ill-gotten kingship and, thus, he contracts two murderers to eliminate him from his way. The 'treachery' Banquo refers to before his demise is the betrayal by Macbeth calling him out saying once a comrade-in-arms, now a regicidal usurper. He is referring to how Macbeth betrayed their friendship because of his greed for the throne. The murderers successfully ambush and kill Banquo but his son Fleance escapes ensuring the witches' prophecy as well as Macbeth's paranoia.

(ii) In Act IV of the play *'Macbeth'*, the witches' role is pivotal as they invoke apparitions that foretell Macbeth's future, further entrenching his descent into tyranny and madness. Their presence signifies the play's exploration of fate, free will and the influence of supernatural forces on human affairs. The eerie atmosphere created by Shakespeare in the play through the witches' chants, 'Double, double toil and trouble; Fire burn, and cauldron bubble' amidst a dark and foreboding setting, heightens the sense of impending doom and accentuates the themes of moral corruption and the psychological turmoil experienced by Macbeth. This atmosphere is integral to the play's tone emphasising the chaos unleashed by Macbeth's ambition and the malevolent forces at play.

(iii) (a) Act IV of the play *'Macbeth'* serves as a crucial link in the narrative bridging the tyrannical reign of Macbeth with the impending retribution and restoration of order. The act opens with the witches' prophetic visions, which embolden Macbeth with a false sense of invincibility, leading him to commit further atrocities. His descent into despotism is marked by the murder of Macduff's family, an act that epitomises his moral decay and sets the stage for his downfall.

Simultaneously, Act IV also depicts the gathering forces of retribution. Malcolm, Duncan's rightful heir, tests Macduff's loyalty and begins to create an army to challenge Macbeth's rule. This convergence of Malcolm's burgeoning resistance and Macbeth's deepening tyranny reflects the play's central themes of legitimacy and usurpation.

The act also amplifies the play's exploration of psychological torment. Macbeth's interactions with the witches reveal his inner turmoil and growing desperation as he clings to their equivocal words. The stark contrast between Macbeth's unravelling psyche and the consolidating opposition highlights the unsustainable nature of his power.

Thus, Act IV is significant in escalating the tension between Macbeth's oppressive regime and the forces that seek to overthrow it. It foreshadows the inevitable clash that will lead to Macbeth's demise and signals a return to rightful kingship and natural order, aligning with the play's overarching narrative of justice and retribution.

(b) The conversation between Caithness and Angus in Shakespeare's *'Macbeth'* offers a revealing glimpse into the protagonist's deteriorating state and the perception of his rule among the Scottish nobility. They speak of Macbeth in terms that suggest both his tyrannical behaviour and the alienation it has caused. Caithness describes Macbeth's efforts to fortify Dunsinane highlighting his desperation and isolation while Angus comments on how Macbeth's royal title hangs loosely about him, 'like a giant's robe upon a dwarfish thief'.

This dialogue underscores Macbeth's tragic trajectory from a respected nobleman to a despised tyrant. His initial valour and ambition, once seen as virtues, have curdled into a destructive paranoia and an insatiable thirst for power that alienates him from his subjects and allies. The metaphor of ill-fitting garments not only conveys Macbeth's unsuitability for the throne but also reflects the unnaturalness of his ascent to power and the inner emptiness that plagues him despite his outward trappings of authority.

Furthermore, their conversation reveals the erosion of loyalty among Macbeth's own allies foreshadowing his impending downfall. The nobles' readiness to join forces with Malcolm indicates a collective yearning for legitimate leadership and a return to stability. Through this exchange, Shakespeare paints a portrait of Macbeth as a figure consumed by his own hubris, ensnared by the very ambition that once propelled him to greatness but now precipitates his tragic end.

4. (i) In Rabindranath Tagore's short story 'Atithi', the protagonist Tarapada is a wanderer whose travels have a profound impact on his character and abilities. The experiences he gains from his nomadic lifestyle shape him into a resourceful and adaptable individual who is capable of navigating the complexities of life with ease. His travels teach him various skills, such as swimming and reading people, which not only ensure his survival but also endow him with a certain charm and independence.

Tarapada's journey instils in him a sense of freedom and self-reliance that contrasts sharply with the more sedentary characters in the story. His skills, acquired through diverse encounters and challenges, reflect his resilience and ability to thrive in changing circumstances. However, these same travels also imbue him with a restlessness that ultimately prevents him from settling down highlighting the double-edged nature of his existence. Through Tarapada, Tagore explores the theme of wanderlust and its impact on human development suggesting that, while travel can enrich one's character, it can also foster an insatiable longing for new horizons.

(ii) In Satyajit Ray's story 'Indigo', Aniruddha awakens in the Dak Bungalow, at night, to find himself in a transformed reality. His appearance has changed; he is now dressed in old-fashioned clothes, his hands are pale, he feels as if his face is thinner and longer, and he even grows thick sideburns. His surroundings also have similarly altered to reflect a bygone era. The decrepit bungalow is now restored to its former glory, lively and well-maintained. Outside, the once overgrown and neglected surroundings have been replaced by well-kept gardens and the fields of indigo. This disconcerting shift not only alters Aniruddha's appearance but also his temporal setting, thrusting him into a historical period of indigo plantations. The stark contrast between his modern self and the colonial environment highlights the story's central motif of time slip leaving Aniruddha to navigate a world that is both familiar and alien, and blurring the lines between reality and illusion.

(iii) (a) In Philip K. Dick's 'The Cookie Lady', the story concludes with a chilling revelation that Mrs. Drew, the seemingly harmless old woman, is a malevolent entity preying on the life force of young Bubber, the innocent schoolboy. The ending is a portrayal of innocence corrupted by sinister forces, emblematic of Dick's recurring themes of deception and the nature of reality.

However, the story could have ended differently. A more optimistic conclusion could have seen Bubber escaping Mrs. Drew's clutches, perhaps through an act of self-awareness or intervention by another character, like his father or his mother. Such an ending would shift the focus from the inevitability of predation to the triumph of innocence and resilience.

However, Dick's choice to end the story with a grim twist is deliberate as it forces the reader to confront the uncomfortable truth that evil often masquerades as benignity. It serves as a cautionary tale about trust and the loss of innocence leaving a lasting impact that a more conventional happy ending might not achieve. The story's conclusion is consistent with Dick's exploration of darker themes and his penchant for leaving readers unsettled prompting reflection on the complexities of human nature and morality.

(b) 'There Will Come Soft Rains' by Ray Bradbury is a unique narrative in that it lacks human characters, despite being a story about humanity's impact. The main 'character' is arguably the automated house which continues its daily routine despite the absence of its human occupants who have been wiped out by a nuclear catastrophe. The house itself is personified through the detailed description of its functions and the care it continues to provide as if in denial of the desolation that has befallen the world outside its walls.

Evidence of the house's central role is found in its meticulous attention to time and the needs of its former residents, from preparing meals to cleaning, everything is carried out with precision and care. The house's systems are described with such personality and purpose that they take on a life of their own becoming a stand-in for the human life that has been wiped out.

The writer's choice to centre the story around the mechanised house serves as a powerful commentary on humanity's reliance on technology and the eerie persistence of our creations even after we are gone. The house's relentless adherence to routine in the face of oblivion sheds light on the futility of human endeavours in the grand scheme of nature and time. Thus, while there are no traditional characters, the house itself becomes a poignant symbol of humanity's transient existence and its footprint on the world.

5. (i) In John Donne's poem 'Death Be Not Proud', the poet employs a range of linguistic devices to diminish the power of death and assert its ultimate impotence. The speaker's lack of fear stems from the personification of death as a boastful yet powerless figure, one that is not so much to be feared as pitied. Donne uses paradoxes, such as describing death as a form of 'sleep' that leads to eternal life, thereby stripping it of its finality and terror.

The poem culminates with an emphatic couplet that delivers a powerful blow to the concept of death's dominance: 'And death shall be no more; Death, thou shalt die.' This bold declaration leaves the readers with a sense of triumph and reassurance reinforcing the Christian belief in the afterlife and the soul's immortality. Donne's masterful use of rhetorical devices challenges the reader's preconceptions about death transforming it from a dreaded end to a mere passage to a greater existence.

(ii) In Mamang Dai's poem 'Small Towns and the River', the collective consciousness of small-town inhabitants is captured through a lens of apprehension and hope. The line 'Small towns growing with anxiety for the future' reflects a communal sentiment of uncertainty and concern as these towns expand and face the unknown prospects of change and development. This anxiety is placed side-by-side with a deep-rooted connection to their environment and traditions, symbolised by the enduring presence of the river.

The theme of the poem revolves around the tension between progress and preservation highlighting how small towns grapple with the desire to grow while maintaining their unique identities. The river serves as a metaphor for continuity amidst change representing both the challenges and the enduring spirit of the communities that reside alongside it. Dai's portrayal of these townsfolk conveys a shared consciousness that is at once wary of what lies ahead yet resilient in the face of inevitable transformation.

(iii) (a) Alfred Tennyson's poem 'Tithonus' speaks to the human condition and the natural laws that govern our existence. The central lesson that society can learn from Tithonus's plight is the acceptance of mortality as an intrinsic part of life. Tithonus, granted eternal life but not eternal youth by the gods, finds himself trapped in an endless cycle of ageing without the release of death. His existence becomes a burden, a poignant reminder that life without an end is not a blessing but a curse.

The poem teaches us that the natural order, including death, has its place and purpose. It warns against the hubris of desiring to transcend our human limitations and disrupt the balance of nature. As a society, we often strive for progress and longevity yet Tennyson's narrative urges us to consider the consequences of such desires. It highlights the importance of living a full and meaningful life within the time we are given, rather than seeking to extend it indefinitely.

The poem 'Tithonus' also reflects on the value of cherishing each moment and embracing the natural cycle of life and death. It serves as a cautionary tale about the perils of tampering with nature's design and encourages a collective understanding that some boundaries are not meant to be crossed. In essence, Tennyson's work imparts wisdom on the acceptance of our mortality as a key to living harmoniously within the tapestry of life.

(b) Wole Soyinka's 'Telephone Conversation' is a powerful indictment of society's superficial and unattainable beauty standards and the deep-seated racial prejudice that often underpins them. The poem narrates an exchange between a Black (African) man and a White (British) landlady, with the man's skin colour becoming the focal point of scrutiny. Soyinka employs irony and satire to expose the absurdity of judging individuals based on their appearance, particularly skin colour.

The poem's dialogue reveals society's unattainable beauty standards, where whiteness is often equated with beauty and desirability, marginalising those who do not fit this narrow criterion. This prejudice is not only superficial but also deeply harmful as it perpetuates discrimination and social exclusion.

Soyinka's use of vivid imagery and conversational tone captures the insidious nature of racial bias highlighting its impact on people's lives. The man's self-deprecating humour in response to the landlady's questions underscores the psychological toll of such encounters. 'Telephone Conversation' thus critiques societal attitudes towards beauty and race, calling for a reevaluation of our values and the recognition of the inherent dignity and worth of every individual, regardless of their physical attributes because people should be valued for their virtue and not something superficial and temporary like their appearance.

SQP Code : **PB-5/10** Series ***i*-Succeed 5-25/10** Roll No.

Sample Question Paper 05

Literature in English 12th (Code 801)

General Instructions

1. It has 5 questions in all.
2. Answer all questions.
3. While answering Question 1 in Section A, you are required to write only ONE option as the correct answer.
4. Internal choice has been given in the long answer questions on Drama, Prose and Poetry.
5. Do not exceed the prescribed word limit while answering the questions in Section B.
6. The intended marks for questions are given in brackets [ ].

Time : 3 Hrs.

Max. Marks : 80

Section A (20 Marks)

Question 1.

Choose the correct option for the following questions. (10)

(i) What do you infer from the lines "Naught's had, all's spent, Where our desire is got without content" from Act III of *Macbeth*? [Interpret]

(a) The speaker is content with their achievements
(b) The speaker is not content with the results
(c) The speaker desires more rewards
(d) The speaker regrets their actions

(ii) How do the Witches sense that someone was coming towards them in Act IV of *Macbeth*? [Understanding]

(a) Twitching of the eye
(b) Pricking of the nose
(c) Pricking of the thumb
(d) Tinkling of the ear

(iii) What are Macbeth's emotions towards Banquo based on the acts studied? [Understanding]

(a) He considers him a friend
(b) He considers him a threat
(c) He is indifferent towards him
(d) He likes Banquo as a brother

(iv) In Act V, what does Macbeth call his frightened servants? [Recall]

(P) Pea-brained
(Q) Chicken-hearted
(R) Cream-faced loon
(S) Lily-livered

(a) (P) and (Q)
(b) (Q) and (R)
(c) (R) and (S)
(d) (P) and (S)

(v) In the story 'There Will Come Soft Rains', what was the fear or urgency of the 'voice'? [Analysis]

Statement I In the living room the voice-clock sang, Tick-tock, seven o'clock, time to get up, time to get up, seven o'clock! as if it were afraid that nobody would.

Statement II The clock ticked on, repeating and repeating its sounds into the emptiness.

(a) Statement I and II are similar.

(b) Statement I and II are not related to each other.

(c) Statement II is the reason for Statement I.

(d) Statement I is the reason for Statement II.

(vi) What is the genre of the story 'Indigo' written by Satyajit Ray? [Understanding]

(a) Mystery (b) Horror and Fantasy

(c) Romance (d) Realism

(vii) What reason does the doctor give when Grandpa fainted in the story 'The Medicine Bag'? [Interpret]

(a) Asthma (b) Cardiac arrest

(c) Stroke (d) Heat exhaustion

(viii) What moral lesson does the poem 'Tithonus' teach us? [Understanding]]

(a) Importance of natural cycle of life and death (b) The beauty of immortality

(c) Significance of love (d) Appreciating the nature

(ix) What is the metaphor used for a character's artistic struggle in the poem, 'Beethoven'? [Recall]

(a) The Piano (b) The Broken record

(c) The Symphony (d) The Audience

(x) According to the poem 'Small Towns and the River', which direction are the dead pointing to? [Recall]

(a) East (b) West

(c) South (d) North

Question 2.

Complete the following sentences by providing a reason for each in brief. Do not write the question. (10)

SP-05

(i) In Act III, Banquo believes that Macbeth had played foul because .... [Understanding]

(ii) In Act III Scene 3, Macbeth decides to send a third murderer to kill Banquo and Fleance because .... [Analysis]

(iii) After their meeting with Hecate, there seems a change in the witches' attitude because .... [Understanding]

(iv) In Act V Scene 1, the woman does not tell the doctor what Lady Macbeth says in her sleep because .... [Recall]

(v) In the story 'The Medicine Bag', Grandpa decided to visit Iowa because .... [Recall]

(vi) In the story, 'Atithi', Motilal Babu agreed to arrange for an English tutor for Tarapada because .... [Analysis]

(vii) In the story 'Indigo', Aniruddha did not get a driver to drive him at night because .... [Recall]

(viii) The river is said to have a soul in the poem 'Small Towns and the River' because .... [Understanding]

(ix) Beethoven's hearing loss becomes a metaphor in the poem because .... [Analysis]

(x) In the poem 'Tithonus', immortality has become a curse for the speaker because .... [Recall]

Section B *(60 Marks)*

Macbeth-William Shakespeare

Question 3

(i) In Act III of the play, how does Macbeth react to Macduff not attending his banquet? Give your answer in 100-150 words including the following details. [Understanding] (5)

(a) Macbeth's character in relation to this reaction

(b) Significance of this moment in the play

(ii) Based on Act IV of *Macbeth*, describe the meeting between Macduff, Malcolm and Ross. Incorporating the following details, give your answer in 100-150 words. [Evaluate] (5)

(a) The effect of this meeting

(b) Macbeth's fortune

(iii) (a) Comment on Shakespeare's clever use of various linguistic devices to draw the attention of the readers, based on the acts studied. Give your answer in 200-250 words. [Analysis] (10)

Or

(b) Analyse Lady Macduff's character in contrast with that of Lady Macbeth based on the acts studied. Write the answer in 200-250 words. [Analysis]

Prism-A Collection of Short Stories

Question 4.

SP-05

(i) In the story 'Atithi', how did Tarapada win the hearts of the villagers? Incorporating the following details, write the answer in 100-150 words. [Understanding] (5)

(a) Tarapada'a interactions with the villagers

(b) Influence of Tarapada's travels on his behaviour

(ii) In the story 'The Medicine Bag', how had Martin described his Grandpa to his friends? Including the following details, give your answer in 100-150 words. [Understanding] (5)

(a) Grandpa's appearance as per Martin's description

(b) Grandpa's behaviour

(iii) (a) Discuss Bubber's motivation to visit Mrs. Drew so frequently while the other neighbourhood kids were afraid of her in the story 'The Cookie Lady'. Also, evaluate how Bubber's greed and his parents' negligence led him to a sad end. Give your answer in 200-250 words. [Evaluate] (10)

Or

(b) Based on your reading of the story 'Indigo' by Satyajit Ray, comment on the 'supernatural' element in the story. Give your answer in 200-250 words. [Analysis]

Rhapsody-Poetry

Question 5.

(i) In the poem 'Small Towns and the River', why does the poet say "Small towns grow with anxiety for the future"? [Analysis] (5)

(a) The significance of this line

(b) The consciousness of people of the small towns

(ii) In the poem 'Death Be Not Proud', how does the poet share his feelings about 'death'? Incorporate the following details and write your answer in 100-150 words. [Understanding] (5)

(a) Cite a significant example sharing this feeling from the poem

(b) The literary device used to emphasise this

(iii) (a) In the poem 'Telephone Conversation', what is the significance of the landlady mentioning that she lives 'off premises'? Discuss in 200-250 words. [Understanding] (10)

Or

(b) Based on your understanding of the poem 'Beethoven', evaluate the use of the recurring phrase 'NOT GOOD ENOUGH' by the poet. Comment on its impact on Beethoven. Write your answer in 200-250 words. [Evaluate]

Answers in Topper's Style

1. (i) (b) The speaker is not content with the results
(ii) (c) Pricking of the thumb
(iii) (b) He considers him a threat
(iv) (c) (R) and (S)
(v) (d) Statement I is the reason for Statement II.
(vi) (b) Horror and fantasy
(vii) (d) heat exhaustion
(viii) (a) Importance of natural cycle of life and death
(ix) (b) The Broken record
(x) (b) West

2. (i) The knew that, after hearing the witches' prophecies, Macbeth had taken the initiative to ensure his kingship
(ii) he couldn't take a chance and risk failing the murder attempt as he did not trust anyone
(iii) earlier they seemed to help Macbeth but now they were preparing for his doom
(iv) she did not want to get involved or become a witness of the secrets that Lady Macbeth was revealing as she sleepwalked
(v) he felt lonely after his grandchildren had left after their yearly visit and he also wanted to see where they lived
(vi) he could see the urge to learn in Tarapada's eyes and wanted to help him
(vii) he was confident about his driving skills and liked to travel alone
(viii) it possesses an understanding of the town's history that symbolises a sentient force that comprehends the cycles of life
(ix) the isolation and struggle he faced in his artistic pursuit emphasises the physical and emotional toll on the musician
(x) it is accompanied by eternal ageing without the release of death

3. (i) In Act III, Macbeth's reaction to Macduff's absence from the banquet reveals his deepening paranoia and his tyrannical grip on power. This reaction shows Macbeth's descent into despotism as he views Macduff's non-attendance as an act of defiance that must be addressed. Macbeth's resolve to confront Macduff signifies his willingness to eliminate any perceived threats to his authority showcasing a character increasingly consumed by suspicion and the need for control.

The significance of this moment lies in its foreshadowing of the conflict between Macbeth and Macduff which becomes central to the play's climax. It also marks a turning point where Macbeth transitions from being a troubled ruler to one who actively seeks out and punishes disloyalty setting the stage for his ultimate downfall.

(ii) In Act IV of *Macbeth*, the meeting between Macduff, Malcolm, and Ross in England is pivotal. Malcolm tests Macduff's loyalty fearing he might be a spy for Macbeth. Once assured of Macduff's sincerity, they plan to unite against Macbeth. Ross brings news of Scotland's suffering under Macbeth's tyranny and later reveals the tragic murder of Macduff's family which drives Macduff into action.

This meeting significantly affects Macbeth's fortune by consolidating opposition against him. It marks the turning point where Malcolm gains the support needed to challenge Macbeth's rule. The union of Malcolm and Macduff, fueled by personal loss and nationalistic fervour, sets the stage for Macbeth's eventual downfall.

(iii) (a) In Acts III, IV, and V of '*Macbeth*', Shakespeare employs a range of linguistic devices to captivate his audience. Act III utilises dramatic irony to great effect; the readers are privy to Macbeth's treachery while Banquo suspects nothing. This creates a tension that keeps the readers on edge. The banquet scene, where Macbeth sees Banquo's ghost, showcases Shakespeare's skill in blending the supernatural with psychological horror using vivid imagery to depict Macbeth's guilt-ridden hallucinations.

Act IV features a shift in language as Malcolm tests Macduff's loyalty through deceitful claims about his own character. This use of deception adds complexity to the dialogue and deepens the audience's understanding of Malcolm's cautious nature. The tragic news of Macduff's family delivered by Ross evokes pathos, effectively drawing the audience into the emotional turmoil of the characters.

In Act V, Lady Macbeth's sleepwalking scene is a linguistic triumph revealing her inner torment througph fragmented speech and obsessive references to blood and handwashing. Her disjointed language contrasts sharply with earlier acts highlighting her mental breakdown.

Shakespeare's clever use of language throughout these acts ensures that the readers are not merely observers but emotionally engaged participants in the unfolding tragedy. The linguistic devices employed, ranging from irony to imagery and fragmented speech, serve to draw attention not only to the action on stage but also to the psychological depth of the characters making 'Macbeth' a compelling experience for its readers.

(b) Lady Macduff and Lady Macbeth are contrasting figures in Shakespeare's *Macbeth*, each embodying different aspects of femininity and morality. Lady Macduff is portrayed as a domestic figure, deeply concerned with the well-being of her family. Her character is rooted in maternal instincts and loyalty, as seen in her interactions with her son and her distress over Macduff's departure to England which she interprets as abandonment.

In stark contrast, Lady Macbeth is driven by ambition and power. Her character represents a departure from traditional gender roles; she is assertive, dominant and unafraid to wield power. While Lady Macduff's world revolves around her family, Lady Macbeth's world revolves around the throne and power. The former is a victim of the play's tragic events suffering the loss of her family due to Macbeth's tyranny. The latter, however, is an architect of her own downfall, with her guilt manifesting in madness and ultimately leading to her suicide.

Shakespeare uses these two characters as foils to each other to explore themes of power, gender and morality. Lady Macduff's innocence and familial devotion sharply contrast with Lady Macbeth's ruthless ambition providing a commentary on the consequences of unchecked desire for power. While both women suffer tragic ends, Lady Macduff's death is undeserved and evokes sympathy as she is a collateral damage in Macbeth's quest for power. Lady Macbeth's demise, however, is the result of her own machinations and the psychological unravelling that follows.

4. (i) In Rabindranath Tagore's story 'Atithi', Tarapada wins the hearts of the villagers through his free-spirited nature and his engaging interactions with them. His travels have instilled in him a sense of independence and a charismatic demeanour which makes him curious about life and that endears him to the villagers. Tarapada's stories of his adventures and his carefree attitude towards life bring a sense of excitement and novelty to the villagers' otherwise monotonous routines. His ability to connect with people from all walks of life, coupled with his youthful exuberance, allows him to form genuine bonds with the villagers leaving a lasting impression on their hearts.

(ii) In 'The Medicine Bag', Martin had his friends believe that his Grandpa was as glamorous as the Indians his friends had seen on TV, with long braided hair, and having a tall and strong stature. Both Martin and his sister, Cheryl never showed any pictures of their Grandpa to their friends as they knew that their Grandpa wouldn't match their imagination or expectations.

Martin's portrayal of his Grandpa's behaviour is less detailed but it is implied that he carries a sense of traditional dignity and cultural significance, especially in the context of passing down the medicine bag—a powerful symbol of heritage. This description serves to create an image of Grandpa that is both venerable and somewhat mystical, reflecting the respect and awe Martin feels towards him.

(iii) (a) Bubber's frequent visits to Mrs. Drew, despite the fear she instils in other neighbourhood kids, stems from a combination of naivety and greed. Unlike his peers, Bubber is lured by the promise of fresh, warm cookies, his favourite snack which Mrs. Drew provides along with cold milk. This indulgence overshadows any trepidation he might feel. While the other children are wary of the old lady and avoid her, Bubber's innocence and desire for cookies blind him to any potential danger.

His greed, coupled with a lack of parental supervision, blinds him to the perils of visiting Mrs. Drew. As the story unfolds, it becomes clearer that Mrs. Drew's intentions are malevolent; she uses Bubber to rejuvenate herself by draining his youth and vitality. His innocence is hence exploited by Mrs. Drew. Bubber's tragic end is a direct result of his unchecked desires and the negligence of his parents who fail to guide and protect him. This narrative serves as a cautionary tale about the perils of greed and the importance of parental responsibility in safeguarding children from harm.

(b) In 'Indigo' by Satyajit Ray, the supernatural element is central to the narrative as it creates an atmosphere of mystery and suspense. The story unfolds through the first-person account of Aniruddha who encounters a haunting experience in an old bungalow. This encounter with the paranormal is described with such vividness that it blurs the line between reality and the supernatural. Ray masterfully uses the supernatural as a device to explore human psychology and fear of the unknown. As mentioned in the beginning of the story, Aniruddha had been intently reading about the 19th century Indigo Plantations of Bengal and Bihar and had been immensely invested in doing so. His deep interest in the topic sets the stage for his encounter with the supernatural. This historical context enriches the narrative as Aniruddha's knowledge of the past becomes intertwined with his present experiences in the bungalow. His investment in this period of history suggests a predisposition to connect with the past which may make him more susceptible to the haunting occurrences he faces. The indigo plantations, with their dark history of exploitation and suffering, provide a fitting backdrop for a tale of haunting as they evoke a sense of lingering spirits and unresolved past traumas. Aniruddha's scholarly pursuit thus becomes a bridge between the logical and the paranormal highlighting Satyajit Ray's skill in weaving historical depth into a supernatural story.

5. (i) In Mamang Dai's poem 'Small Towns and the River', the line "Small towns grow with anxiety for the future" reflects the collective apprehension of small-town residents about their uncertain futures. The significance of this line lies in its portrayal of small towns as places where life is intimately connected with the cycles of nature and mortality. The townspeople are acutely aware of the fragility of life as they frequently encounter news of death which casts a shadow over their existence.

This line also speaks to the consciousness of small-town inhabitants suggesting a deep-seated concern for what lies ahead. Unlike the river, which symbolises eternal life and continuity, the people are burdened with the knowledge of their mortality and the transience of human existence.

Their anxiety is not only about personal futures but also about the legacy and survival of their community in the face of inevitable change.

(ii) In John Donne's poem 'Death Be Not Proud', the poet challenges the conventional perception of death. The lines "From rest and sleep, which but thy pictures be, Much pleasure; then from thee much more must flow" convey two very important aspects relating to the poet's feelings about death.

Donne's feelings about 'death' in the poem are paradoxical. He personifies death as an ephemeral entity defying its supposed power. The poet suggests that death is merely a transition and a temporary state akin to rest or sleep.

The imagery of 'pictures' implies that death is a mere reflection or shadow of existence. Donne views death as an intermediary stage before something greater unfolds.

The literary device employed here is paradox. By placing 'rest and sleep' with 'much pleasure' and emphasising that 'much more must flow' from death, the poet subverts the traditional fear associated with dying. He implies that death leads to an even more profound experience, perhaps eternal life or even spiritual awakening. The paradox highlights the poem's central theme, which states the triumph of the soul over mortality.

(iii) (a) The landlady initially appears pleasant but her demeanour changes abruptly when the speaker reveals he is African. Although she had advertised the room without racial restrictions, her true feelings emerge soon.

By emphasising that she lives 'off premises,' she implies that her personal space remains separate from the property she rents out. This distinction suggests hidden prejudice in which she doesn't want to share her immediate living environment with someone of a different race. The power dynamic becomes evident when her assertion of living 'off premises' establishes an imbalance. She holds the upper hand in this transaction. Her refusal to engage directly with the speaker's racial identity reinforces her authority. The silence that follows his confession further shows her control over the conversation. Meanwhile, the speaker's plea, 'I hate a wasted journey', reveals his vulnerability. He desperately seeks acceptance but the landlady's discriminatory stance leaves him at her mercy.

Throughout the poem, the poet masterfully employs irony and satire. The mundane act of seeking accommodation becomes an example of societal prejudice. The landlady's hypocrisy, publicly claiming non-discrimination while privately revealing her bias, exposes the absurdity of racial discrimination. The telephone, a symbol of communication, becomes a conduit for both connection and division here. With each word exchanged, the power dynamic shifts leaving the reader to contemplate the complexities of racial bias even in seemingly mundane interactions.

(b) In the context of a poem about 'Beethoven', the recurring phrase 'NOT GOOD ENOUGH' serves as a powerful motif reflecting the relentless self-criticism and pursuit of perfection that often characterises great artists.

For Beethoven, who was known for his exacting standards and constant revision of his compositions, such a phrase might echo the internal struggle between his creative aspirations and his critical self-evaluation.

The repetition of 'NOT GOOD ENOUGH' could symbolise the incessant drive for artistic excellence that propels Beethoven's work while also highlighting the personal toll of such ambition. It may underscore the distinction between public adulation and private dissatisfaction suggesting that, despite his success, Beethoven never fully satisfied his own harshest critic.

This phrase's impact on Beetho-ven within the poem could be multifaceted. On one hand, it might fuel his determination to surpass his previous achievements leading to greater heights of musical innovation. On the other hand, it could also represent an internal barrier, a voice of doubt that haunts him, like his father's expectations, which could never be satisfied, perhaps contributing to his feelings of isolation or despair.

Overall, 'NOT GOOD ENOUGH' could be interpreted as both a curse and a catalyst within Beethoven's life encapsulating the paradox of a genius who is revered by others yet relentlessly driven by an unattainable ideal of perfection.

SQP Code : **PB-6/10**	Series *i*-**Succeed 6-25/10**	Roll No.								

Sample Question Paper 06

Literature in English 12th (Code 801)

General Instructions

1. It has 5 questions in all.
2. Answer all questions.
3. While answering Question 1 in Section A, you are required to write only ONE option as the correct answer.
4. Internal choice has been given in the long answer questions on Drama, Prose and Poetry.
5. Do not exceed the prescribed word limit while answering the questions in Section B.
6. The intended marks for questions are given in brackets [ ].

Time : 3 Hrs.

Max. Marks : 80

Section A *(20 Marks)*

Question 1.

Choose the correct option for the following questions. (10)

(i) In Act III, Scene 2 of the play, Macbeth says "deed of dreadful note". What do you think he is referring to by saying this? [Understanding]

(a) Banquo and Fleance's murder (b) Macbeth's coronation

(c) Murder of Duncan (d) The Banquet

(ii) Based on Act IV of the play, what did Ross compare his and others' situation with? [Recall]

(a) Crossing a vast desert

(b) Swimming in the mighty river

(c) Floating upon a wild and violent sea

(d) Diving in deep dark waters

(iii) What is the figure of speech used in the following lines from Act IV of *Macbeth*? [Understanding]

"This comfort with the like. But I have words that would be howled out in the desert air, where hearing should not latch them"

(a) Metaphor (b) Alliteration

(c) Simile (d) Apostrophe

(iv) In Act III of *Macbeth*, which of the following events take place? [Recall]

(P) Lennox's comments upon Macbeth's 'official' versions violent deaths

(Q) News of Macduff's flight to England

(R) Death of Lady Macbeth

(S) Movement of Birnam Woods

(a) (P) and (Q) (b) (R) and (S)

(c) (P) and (S) (d) (Q) and (R)

(v) Read the two statements from the short story 'Atithi' and choose the correct option from the ones given below. [Analysis]

Statement I Tarapada took over and soon had the dish ready and had cooked some vegetables too with practised skill.

Statement II Tarapada was the darling of all; mother, brothers, sisters and neighbours doted on him.

(a) Statement I and II are similar. (b) Statement I and II are not related to each other.

(c) Statement II is the reason for Statement I. (d) Statement I is the reason for Statement II.

(vi) In the short story 'The Cookie Lady', who forbade Bubber from visiting Mrs. Drew? [Recall]

(a) Bubber's friends (b) Bubber's father

(c) Bubber's mother (d) Bubber's teacher

(vii) From the short story 'Indigo', why did Aniruddha want to visit his friend? [Analysis]

(a) It was Promode's wedding

(b) He wished to get away from home for the weekend

(c) His friend was ill

(d) He missed his friend

(viii) What literary device has been employed in the given lines from the poem 'Telephone Conversation'? [Understanding]

"HOW DARK?"... I had not misheard ... "ARE YOU LIGHT

OR VERY DARK"?

(a) Repetition (b) Simile

(c) Hyperbole (d) Metaphor

(ix) In the poem 'Death Be Not Proud', what is the tone like? [Interpret]

SP-06

(a) Fearful (b) Angry

(c) Severe (d) Melancholic

(x) Based on the poem 'Small Towns and the River', what do tuberoses signify? [Understanding]

(a) Eternal life (b) Agriculture and related practice

(c) Rituals related to nature (d) Transient nature of life

Question 2.

Complete the following sentences by providing a reason for each in brief. Do not write the question. (10)

(i) In the play *Macbeth*, the second murderer lets the third murderer join them because .... [Recall]

(ii) In Act III of the play, according to Lennox, Macbeth had killed Duncan's guards because .... [Understanding]

(iii) According to the second apparition, Macbeth was told to live to 'scorn the power of man' because .... [Analysis]

(iv) Macbeth thinks of the apparitions as 'sweet bodements' because .... [Analysis]

(v) In the story 'Atithi', Charushashi's character was like a puzzle because .... [Understanding]

(vi) In the story, 'The Cookie Lady' Mrs. Drew has been compared to 'weeds in the garden' because .... [Interpret]

(vii) In the story 'There Will Come Soft Rains', the robotic mice were angry because .... [Recall]

(viii) According to the poem 'Small Towns and the River', the dead are placed pointing West because .... [Recall]

(ix) Beethoven removed the legs of his piano because .... [Analysis]

(x) In the poem 'Death Be Not Proud', the speaker rejects the notion of death's control over humanity because .... [Understanding]

Section B *(60 Marks)*

Macbeth-William Shakespeare

Question 3.

(i) How has Shakespeare used irony in Act III Scene 4 to heighten the tension and suspense? Including the following points, write your answer in 100-150 words. [Understanding] (5)

(a) Macbeth's plan to kill Banquo

(b) His inner turmoil

(ii) Based on the reading of acts prescribed, discuss the distinguishing features about Malcolm's personality. Including the following points, write your answer in 100-150 words. [Evaluate] (5)

(a) His reaction to his father's murder

(b) His plan to avenge Duncan's death

(iii) (a) How does Lady Macduff's fate differ from that of Lady Macbeth? Discuss in 200-250 words. [Evaluate] (10)

Or

(b) How does Macduff react to the news of his family's murder? Discuss in 200-250 words. [Evaluate]

SP-06

Prism-A Collection of Short Stories

Question 4.

(i) Based on the story 'Indigo', describe Aniruddha Bose's car journey and the destination he was ultimately led to, including the following points, in 100-150 words. [Analysis] (5)

(a) The 'signs' he got before his journey

(b) People who helped him along the way

(ii) What role do the other children play in warning Bubber about Mrs. Drew in the story' The Cookie Lady'? Incorporating the following details, write your answer in 100-150 words. [Understanding] (5)

(a) Clues and hints given by the children about Mrs. Drew's true nature

(b) Bubber's ignorance

(iii) (a) Based on the story 'Atithi', comment on Tarapada's extended stay at Motilal Babu's in contrast with his nature of not staying at one place for a long time. Give your answer in 200-250 words. [Analysis] (10)

Or

(b) Evaluate the importance of the title of the story 'There Will Come Soft Rains' being taken from Sara Teasdale's poem of the same name. Write your answer in 200-250 words. [Evaluate]

Rhapsody-Poetry

Question 5.

(i) In the poem 'Small Towns and the River', how is the event of 'death' described by Mamang Dai? Including the following points, write your answer in 100-150 words. [Understanding] (5)

(a) The river has a soul

(b) The tone of the poem

(ii) How has the poet emphasised the 'powerlessness' of death in the poem 'Death Be Not Proud'? Incorporating the following details, give your answer in 100-150 words. [Understanding] (5)

(a) Linguistic devices used in the poem

(b) Comparison of death with sleep

(iii) (a) How does the poem explore Beethoven's personal struggles? Discuss as per your understanding of the poem in 200-250 words. [Interpret] (10)

Or

(b) Based on your understanding of the poem 'Tithonus', discuss in detail how the speaker has expressed his regret of accepting the 'gift' of immortality in 200-250 words. [Analysis]

Answers *in Topper's Style*

1. (i) (a) Banquo and Fleance's murder
(ii) (c) Floating upon a wild and violent sea
(iii) (d) Apostrophe
(iv) (a) (P) and (Q)
(v) (b) Statement I and II are not related to each other.
(vi) (b) Bubber's father
(vii) (b) He wished to get away from home for the weekend
(viii) (a) Repetition
(ix) (d) Melancholic
(x) (d) Transient nature of life

2. (i) he knew all the plans and the instructions that they had received from Macbeth
(ii) he could not handle his rage and grief. He was angry at them for not being able to protect the king
(iii) no man born of woman could harm him
(iv) he feels they've predicted things to make him feel comfortable
(v) she had peculiar choices in every matter of her life which were usually inconsistent
(vi) of her selfish rejuvenation at the expense of young Bubber's life force and her neglected, shabby house where she lives, with peeling paint and overgrown weeds which mirrors her own decay
(vii) a dirty dog had entered the house and they had to clean the trail of mud left by him everywhere
(viii) it shows anticipation of the soul's journey into the golden East, symbolising a transition
(ix) he was seeking a direct, physical connection with music and this action emphasised the intensity of his devotion to his art
(x) he believes death lacks authority and reaffirms the supremacy of divine providence

3. (i) In Act III, Scene 4 of Shakespeare's *Macbeth*, irony is skillfully employed to intensify tension and suspense. Macbeth, now the reigning king, devises a plan to eliminate Banquo, his former comrade and a perceived threat.

He arranges for murderers to assassinate Banquo and his son, Fleance. The irony lies in Macbeth's false sense of control. Driven by ambition and paranoia, he believes that Banquo's death will secure his throne. However, the witches' prophecies continue to haunt him revealing the limits of his power. Macbeth's desperate attempt to manipulate fate only leads to more chaos and uncertainty.

As the banquet unfolds, Macbeth sees Banquo's ghost which is a display show of his guilt and inner turmoil. The ghost is invisible to others, creating dramatic irony—the readers know of Macbeth's mental torment while the guests remain oblivious. His outbursts and Lady Macbeth's attempts to downplay his behaviour add to the suspense. Macbeth's unravelling psyche contrasts with the facade he presents to the court, heightening the tension. In this scene, irony underscores Macbeth's tragic downfall as his actions and mental state collide with the supernatural forces at play.

(ii) In William Shakespeare's play *Macbeth*, Malcolm, the eldest son of King Duncan, undergoes a significant transformation. Initially, weak, inexperienced and fearful of getting killed, he flees Scotland after his father's murder. However, as the play progresses, we can see that Malcolm matures. With the help of Macduff and the English army, he eventually overthrows Macbeth, retakes the throne and restores the order that was shattered when Duncan was killed. Malcolm represents stability and lawfulness which is in contrast with Macbeth's violent ambitions and apathy towards his people. His determination to avenge Duncan's death and reclaim the rightful throne underscores his commitment to Scotland's well-being and contrasts sharply with Macbeth's bloodthirsty pursuit of power.

(iii) (a) Lady Macduff's fate is a direct consequence of Macbeth's tyranny. She is introduced in Act III, Scene 2 as a domestic figure concerned for her family's safety. Her fate is sealed when Macbeth, in a paranoid bid to secure his throne and power, orders the murder of Macduff's family. Lady Macduff and her son meet a tragic end, becoming victims of Macbeth's senseless violence which marks his descent into madness.

In contrast, Lady Macbeth's fate is largely self-inflicted. Her initial ambition and manipulation lead to her husband's rise to power but, as the play progresses, she becomes consumed by guilt and fear. In Act V, her psychological torment manifests in sleepwalking and obsessive handwashing, symbolising her inability to cleanse herself of the bloodshed she has caused. Ultimately, unable to live with her conscience, Lady Macbeth takes her own life.

While both women suffer tragic ends, Lady Macduff's death is undeserved and evokes sympathy; she is a collateral damage in Macbeth's quest for power. Lady Macbeth's demise, however, is the result of her own machinations and the psychological unravelling that follows. Their contrasting fates underscore the themes of innocence versus guilt and the destructive nature of power and ambition in the play.

(b) Macduff's reaction to the news of his family's murder is one of profound sorrow and grief. In Act IV, Scene 3 of the play, upon learning of the slaughter, he is overwhelmed by a sense of guilt believing that his own actions have led to his family's death rather than any wrongdoing on their part. He expresses this sorrowful sentiment lamenting that they were killed due to his actions.

Macduff's grief is compounded by a sense of responsibility as he feels guilty for leaving his family alone, vulnerable and without any protection while he was away in England. This guilt transforms into a driving force for revenge against Macbeth who ordered the murder of his wife and children. Macduff's emotional turmoil and subsequent quest for vengeance are pivotal in the play as they lead to the ultimate confrontation with Macbeth and contribute to the tyrant's downfall.

The news of his family's murder reveals Macduff's emotional intelligence, his emotional depth and his loyalty towards his own family and towards Scotland. It also serves as a catalyst for his actions later shifting his role from a political figure to a deeply personal one as he seeks justice for his family and his country.

4. (i) In the story 'Indigo', Aniruddha Bose embarks on a fateful car journey. Aniruddha, a twenty-nine-year-old bachelor, had been engrossed in reading about the 19th-century indigo plantations in Bihar and Bengal. His desire to escape city life had led him to buy a car and, when his friend invited him for a visit, he couldn't say no. Despite initial delays caused by neighbours' questions, he set off, starting his journey under a clear blue sky. However, he faced setbacks: a punctured tire, a thunderstorm and another flat tire. Lost and rain-soaked, he realised he had taken a wrong turn and reached a dead end.

Along the way, an old man named Sukhanram offered him shelter in a Dak Bungalow.

The bungalow, once owned by an indigo planter, stood near the factory's remaining chimney. That night, Aniruddha heard a hound scratching at the door. His wristwatch vanished and he experienced some really shocking changes like having pale hands, an Englishman's voice and different clothes. Ultimately, Aniruddha's journey led him to an eerie encounter with the past blurring the boundaries between reality and the supernatural.

(ii) In 'The Cookie Lady', the other children play a peripheral yet significant role in warning Bubber about Mrs. Drew. They taunt him about his visits to the 'cookie lady' hinting at their collective apprehension and the neighbourhood's perception of Mrs. Drew as someone to be avoided. Although their warnings are not direct, their teasing serves as an informal alert to the potential dangers of associating with Mrs. Drew. Bubber, however, dismisses their mockery and continues his visits, driven by his desire for cookies and oblivious to the underlying caution in their words. The children's behaviour reflects a communal sense of unease and serves as a subtle narrative device to foreshadow the ominous events that unfold.

(iii) (a) In the short story 'Atithi' by Rabindranath Tagore, the statement that Tarapada did not stay at one place for long except for his extended stay at Motilal Babu's home holds significant thematic implications. Tarapada, a wandering ascetic, represents the transient nature of life and the impermanence of human connections. His nomadic lifestyle contrasts sharply with the settled existence of Motilal Babu and his family. Tarapada's arrival disrupts the routine of the household introducing an element of unpredictability and spiritual inquiry.

During his two-year stay, Tarapada becomes an integral part of the family and the village sharing meals, stories, helping people around, learning new things and having philosophical discussions. His presence challenges societal norms and materialistic pursuits emphasising the value of spiritual seeking over material possessions. From the members of Motilal Babu's family, to the people of the village, everyone feels touched and in awe of having met Tarapada. Through Tarapada, Tagore explores themes of hospitality, compassion and the search for deeper meaning in life's experiences. Despite his eventual departure, Tarapada leaves an indelible mark on Motilal Babu's family prompting introspection and a reevaluation of their priorities in life. Thus, the statement underscores the transformative power of unexpected encounters and the enduring impact of transient guests in our lives.

(b) The title 'There Will Come Soft Rains' holds profound significance in Ray Bradbury's short story. Derived from Sara Teasdale's poem, which Bradbury references, the title encapsulates the central theme of the narrative. Teasdale's poem, published in 1918, reflects on the aftermath of human extinction due to war, envisioning a world where nature continues its cycles despite humanity's absence. In Bradbury's story, set in a post-apocalyptic future, a mechanised house persists long after its inhabitants have perished in a nuclear catastrophe. The title alludes to the gentle, inevitable return of natural processes like soft rains, blooming flowers, and the passage of time, despite humanity's destructive tendencies. The house, devoid of life, mechanically performs its daily routines: cooking meals, cleaning, reading out birthday/anniversary reminders and maintaining itself. Yet, its mechanical precision contrasts starkly with the absent human touch in the story emphasising the eerie emptiness.

The title serves as a poignant reminder of humanity's impermanence and the resilience of nature. It sheds light on the irony that, while technology endures, the very beings it once served have vanished. This cautionary tale warns against unchecked technological advancement and the potential consequences of human hubris. Hence, the title encapsulates both the haunting beauty of nature's continuity and the tragic absence of human connection throughout the story.

5. (i) In Mamang Dai's poem 'Small Towns and the River', the portrayal of death is both poignant and thought-provoking. The poet juxtaposes the impermanence of human existence with the perpetual flow of the river. The small towns, where every other day brings news of someone's passing, evoking grief and sadness, symbolises mortality. However, the river stands in stark contrast, it lives eternally, its soul intertwined with the passage of time. The concept of an afterlife and the presence of a guiding force offer solace amidst thoughts of death. The tone oscillates between melancholy and acceptance capturing the essence of life's transience and the enduring nature of natural forces.

(ii) In the poem 'Death Be Not Proud', the poet masterfully emphasises the powerlessness of death through linguistic devices and a striking comparison with sleep. Donne personifies death addressing it directly as if it were a conscious being. By calling it 'mighty and dreadful', he mocks its supposed authority. This personification reveals the limitations and vulnerability of death. The comparison of death to 'rest and sleep' is a powerful metaphor. Donne suggests that death is merely a transition, a temporary state akin to restful slumber.

The word 'pictures' implies that death's fearsome reputation is an illusion and what lies beyond is familiar and comforting. The poet even suggests that drugs can induce a similar experience diminishing death's terror. In conclusion, Donne's defiance against death lies in portraying it as a powerless figure, a mere interlude before the soul's eternal awakening.

(iii) (a) In the poem 'Beethoven', his personal struggles are a central theme exploring the tension between his profound musical genius and the challenges he faced. The poem delves into his struggle with deafness, a cruel irony for a composer whose life revolved around sound. This adversity is portrayed as both a source of deep despair and a catalyst for extraordinary creativity, compelling him to compose by internal hearing rather than external sound.

The poem also reflects on Beethoven's turbulent personal life including his fraught relationships, hard childhood, his physical limitations and his sense of isolation. It examines how these struggles influenced his music infusing it with emotional depth and complexity. The recurring phrase 'NOT GOOD ENOUGH' underscores these themes representing the relentless self-doubt and pressure Beethoven placed on himself to achieve perfection despite, or perhaps because of, his hardships.

Beethoven's defiance against his fate, particularly his refusal to be silenced by his deafness, could be another aspect explored in the poem. His determination to continue composing even as his hearing deteriorated might be depicted as both heroic and tragic, a testament to the indomitable spirit of an artist facing insurmountable odds.

Overall, the poem portrays Beethoven's personal struggles as inextricably linked to his creative process, painting a portrait of a man whose greatest works were born from the depths of his suffering and resilience.

(b) 'Tithonus', a dramatic monologue by Alfred Lord Tennyson, explores the consequences of immortality. The poem centres on Tithonus, a mortal man who was granted eternal life by the goddess Aurora (Eos). However, this divine gift turns into a curse, leading Tithonus to express profound regret. Through vivid imagery and introspection, Tennyson delves into themes of love, time, and the human condition.

Tithonus' begins by reminiscing about his past—a time when he was chosen by Aurora. His beauty once rivalled that of the gods but now he is a mere shadow of his former self. The 'falling woods' and 'weeping vapours' symbolise decay emphasising the relentless erosion of his mortal beauty. Immortality has robbed him of vitality, leaving him trapped in perpetual ageing.

Tithonus' lament extends beyond physical decay. He grapples with the cruelty of immortality itself. Unlike the gods, who remain eternally youthful, Tithonus exists in a twilight state—neither fully alive nor dead. His plea to Aurora 'take back thy gift' reveals desperation. Immortality has severed him from the natural order, rendering him an anomaly.

Thus, Tennyson's 'Tithonus' serves as a cautionary tale. Immortality, once coveted, becomes a burden. Tithonus' regret reflects the paradox that eternal life devoid of vitality is no life at all. Through this poem, Tennyson invites readers to reflect on the price of immortality, a gift that, in the end, exacts a heavy toll on the human spirit.

SQP Code : **PB-7/10** Series ***i*-Succeed 7-25/10** Roll No.

Sample Question Paper 07

Literature in English 12th (Code 801)

General Instructions

1. It has 5 questions in all.
2. Answer all questions.
3. While answering Question 1 in Section A, you are required to write only ONE option as the correct answer.
4. Internal choice has been given in the long answer questions on Drama, Prose and Poetry.
5. Do not exceed the prescribed word limit while answering the questions in Section B.
6. The intended marks for questions are given in brackets [ ].

Time : 3 Hrs.
Max. Marks : 80

Section A (20 Marks)

Question 1.

Choose the correct option for the following questions. (10)

(i) Based on your reading of Act III of *Macbeth*, complete the lines using suitable option- [Recall]

'Things without all remedy
Should be without regard...'

(a) It is done as it should be
(b) What's happened is happened
(c) It is for the best
(d) What's done is done

(ii) In Act V of *Macbeth*, what does Macbeth compare life with? [Recall]

(a) A brief candle
(b) The seasons
(c) A dream
(d) An hourglass

(iii) What makes Macbeth doubt the witches' prophecies according to Act V of the play? [Understanding]

(a) The sight of moving forest
(b) Seeing Banquo's ghost
(c) Alliance between Scotland and England
(d) Desertion by his soldiers

(iv) In Act IV of the play, Ross' visit to Lady Macduff was for [Recall]

(P) consoling her and her children
(Q) offering protection to Macduff's family
(R) justifying Macduff's flight to England
(S) trying to convince Lady Macduff

(a) (P) and (Q)
(b) (R) and (S)
(c) (P) and (S)
(d) (Q) and (R)

(v) Read the two statements from the short story 'There Will Come Soft Rains' and choose the correct option from the ones given below. [Analysis]

Statement I The entire West face of the house was black.

Statement II ... the silhoutte in paint of a man mowing a lawn.

(a) Statement I and II are related.
(b) Statement I and II are not related to each other.
(c) Statement II is the reason for Statement I.
(d) Statement I is the reason for Statement II.

(vi) What was the habit that Aniruddha picked when he was in Monghyr? [Recall]

(a) He started drinking alcohol
(b) He had the urge to go away from the hectic life
(c) He started liking solitude
(d) He would frequently leave his house

(vii) Where does Grandpa go to visit his grandchildren in the story 'The Medicine Bag'? [Recall]

(a) California
(b) Bristol
(c) Michigan
(d) Iowa

(viii) According to the poem, Beethoven had a complicated relationship with his [Understanding]

(a) pet
(b) mother
(c) father
(d) brother

(ix) The poem 'Tithonus', talks about the effects of [Analysis]

(a) ageing
(b) immortality
(c) unchecked desires
(d) eternal love

(x) The poem 'Telephone Conversation' is written by [Recall]

(a) Shane Koyczan
(b) Rabindranath Tagore
(c) Wole Soyinka
(d) John Donne

Question 2.

Complete the following sentences by providing a reason for each in brief. Do not write the question. (10)

(i) In Act III of *Macbeth*, Banquo's son Fleance was able to escape the attack because .... [Recall]

SP-07

(ii) When Macduff refuses to return in Act III Scene 6 of *Macbeth*, the messenger looks at him with disapproval because .... [Understanding]

(iii) Lady Macduff calls Macduff a traitor in Act IV because .... [Analysis]

(iv) In Act V, Macbeth says he doesn't fear the 'nightly shriek' because .... [Recall]

(v) In the story 'Indigo', Aniruddha could not forget the twenty-seventh of April because .... [Recall]

(vi) In the story 'Atithi', Charushashi too started taking English lessons with Tarapada because .... [Recall]

(vii) In the story 'The Medicine Bag', the medicine bag was important because .... [Understanding]

(viii) The fish play an important role in the poem 'Small Towns and the River' because .... [Understanding]

(ix) Tithonus received the gift of 'immortality' from his beloved but wasn't happy with it because .... [Analysis]

(x) Beethoven's father seemed to remain unsatisfied with his music because .... [Understanding]

Section B *(60 Marks)*

Macbeth-William Shakespeare

Question 3.

(i) Based on your reading of the acts prescribed, evaluate the statement – 'kings – becoming graces' incorporating the following details, in 100-150 words. [Evaluate] (5)

(a) Malcolm and Macduff's discussion

(b) Macbeth and Duncan as kings

(ii) How does Macbeth react when he hears of the Birnam Forest moving towards his castle? Give your answer in 100-150 words including the following points. [Understanding] (5)

(a) Development of Macbeth's emotions

(b) The reason behind the forest moving

(iii) (a) With appropriate examples from the play, discuss the importance of Macduff's character. Write your answer in 200-250 words. [Analysis] (10)

Or

(b) Even after his gruelling efforts, Macbeth couldn't hold onto the throne. Comment on the statement based on your understanding of the acts studied. Write your answer in 200-250 words. [Analysis]

Prism-A Collection of Short Stories

Question 4.

(i) Discuss the significance of the 'fire' element in the story 'There Will Come Soft Rains'. Including the following details, write your answer in 100-150 words. [Evaluate] (5)

(a) The fire destroyed the house

(b) The mechanised house trying to put the fire out

(ii) Describe the significance of the items within the medicine bag for Martin's family based on the prescribed story 'The Medicine Bag'. Including the following details, write your answer in 100-150 words. [Understanding] (5)

(a) Grandpa's attachment to the medicine bag

(b) Martin's hesitation

(iii) (a) Discuss Motilal Babu's character from the story 'Atithi'. Why do you think Motilal Babu and Annapurna took Tarapada in? Write your answer in 200-250 words. [Analysis] (10)

Or

(b) Discuss the main theme of the story 'The Cookie Lady'. What lesson does the story teach us? Write your answer in 200-250 words. [Understanding]

Rhapsody-Poetry

Question 5.

(i) How is the speaker's confession received by the landlady? Including the following details, write your answer in 100-150 words. [Understanding] (5)

(a) The information it gives about the landlady.

(b) The clever reply given by the speaker

(ii) Comment on the use of imagery in the poem 'Small Towns and the River'. Including the following details, write your answer in 100-150 words. [Analysis] (5)

(a) The beauty of the town

(b) The significance of the river for the people in the town

(iii) (a) What message does the poem 'Death Be Not Proud' convey to the readers? Based on your understanding of the poem, write your answer in 200-250 words. [Understanding] (10)

Or

(b) Based on your reading of the poem 'Beethoven' by Shane Koyczan, give a brief description of Beethoven's relationship with his father. Write the answer in 200-250 words. [Evaluate]

Answers *in Topper's Style*

1. (i) (d) What's done is done
(ii) (a) A brief candle
(iii) (a) The sight of moving forest
(iv) (b) (R) and (S)
(v) (a) Statement I and II are related.
(vi) (b) He had the urge to go away from the hectic life
(vii) (d) Iowa
(viii) (c) father.
(ix) (c) unchecked desires.
(x) (c) Wole Soyinka.

2. (i) it was dark and he used the lack of visibility to his advantage
(ii) the messenger was loyal to Macbeth and told Macduff that he would regret his actions
(iii) he left his family alone without any protection or resources
(iv) he has become aware of horrors of all kinds and nothing seems to startle him now
(v) that's the day Aniruddha started his journey to go meet his friend but ended up experiencing supernatural horror at the Dak Bungalow
(vi) she wanted to become like Tarapada so that she could be his equal and impress her parents
(vii) the bag represents tradition, protection and ancestral connection
(viii) it is symbolic of departed souls, suggesting continuity beyond mortality
(ix) he only received the gift of immortality and not eternal youth due to which he continued to age and suffer the ravages of old age while his beloved stayed young forever
(x) he expected him to create perfect notes and in his desperation to see him as a genius, he never appreciated Beethoven as he was never good enough for him

3. (i) In Act IV, of the play *Macbeth*, Malcolm engages in an impactful and revealing discussion with Macduff. Initially, Malcolm pretends to be morally flawed admitting corruptness to test Macduff's loyalty.

However, in the midst of this act lies a shared commitment to Scotland. Both Malcolm and Macduff prioritise their loyalty to the nation over their personal ambitions. This idealistic perspective of these two men contrasts sharply with Macbeth's power-hungry tyranny. Malcolm's humanity and determination to stop Macbeth, even after losing his own family, highlight his contrast with Macbeth. Ultimately, it is Macduff who kills Macbeth but Malcolm's rightful ascension to the throne reinforces the legitimacy of succession.

From Acts III, IV and V of the play, we understand that King Duncan embodies stability and good leadership. His moral compass sets him apart, but ironically, it also makes him vulnerable. As we know, Duncan's misplaced trust in Macbeth and Cawdor leads to betrayal and his untimely demise. In contrast, Macbeth seizes power through regicide, disrupting the natural order of succession. Duncan's death marks the end of peace and the rise of corruption. Therefore, Macbeth, though a skilled warrior, lacks Duncan's benevolence.

(ii) When Macbeth receives news of Birnam Wood advancing toward Dunsinane Castle, his emotions undergo a tumultuous transformation. Initially, he dismisses the report relying on the prophecy that assured him no man born of woman could harm him. However, as reality sinks in, rage and terror consume him. His defiance wavers and he acknowledges weariness with life. The forest's movement symbolises the fulfilment of the witches' prophecy undermining his false sense of invincibility. Macbeth's desperation intensifies as he realises that his fate is closing in and he resolves to fight to the bitter end. The moving forest represents the camouflage of Malcolm's forces who cut branches to conceal their numbers. Macbeth's emotional turmoil mirrors the impending doom that awaits him, as Birnam Wood inexorably approaches Dunsinane.

(iii) (a) Macduff, a multifaceted character in *Macbeth,* plays a pivotal role that resonate throughout the play. He begins as a loyal noble fighting for King Duncan. His immediate distrust of Macbeth's claim about Duncan's murder sets him apart. Macduff's unwavering loyalty to Scotland and his refusal to attend Macbeth's coronation highlight his commitment to justice and the natural order. His bravery is evident when he confronts Macbeth directly at great personal risk.

Macduff's family becomes a tragic target of Macbeth's wrath. The ruthless murder of Macduff's wife and children (Act IV, Scene 3) propels him into a quest for vengeance. His grief and determination drive the plot forward emphasising the consequences of Macbeth's tyranny. While in England, Macduff becomes a beacon of hope for Scotland, his mission to place Malcolm on the throne represents the restoration of rightful rule. Macduff's actions align with the prophecy that Macbeth can be defeated only by someone 'not of woman born'. His revelation about his birth shatters Macbeth's false sense of invincibility. Thus, Macduff's role in the final battle symbolises justice prevailing over tyranny.

Macduff's loyalty, bravery and unwavering pursuit of justice make him a crucial character. His personal tragedy fuels the larger struggle against Macbeth, ultimately leading to the tyrant's downfall. Macduff embodies the resilience of Scotland and the triumph of honour over ambition. His character serves as a moral compass highlighting the consequences of unchecked power and the importance of rightful leadership.

(b) William Shakespeare's play *Macbeth* unfolds a gripping tale of ambition, treachery and the corrupting influence of power. At the heart of this tragedy lies Macbeth, a once-valiant warrior whose ascent to the throne is marked by ruthless deeds and inner turmoil. However, despite his gruelling efforts, Macbeth ultimately fails to hold onto the throne.

Macbeth's initial murder of King Duncan sets the stage for his descent into guilt-ridden madness. The blood on his hands becomes a metaphor for the weight of his crimes. His hallucinations, like the ghostly appearance of Banquo, reveal a tormented psyche. Macbeth's inability to wash away the metaphorical blood underscores the irreversible nature of his actions.

Macbeth's tyrannical rule destabilised Scotland. His disregard for justice and the natural order alienates the nobles and commoners alike. The murder of Banquo and the Macduff family further fuels opposition. Macbeth's paranoia drives him to eliminate perceived threats but this only accelerates the unravelling of his kingdom. The nobles rally behind Malcolm who represents the rightful heir to the throne. Macbeth's reign becomes synonymous with chaos emphasising the consequences of unchecked ambition.

The three witches serve as catalysts for Macbeth's downfall. Their prophecies initially embolden him promising kingship and invincibility. However, their cryptic warnings sow seeds of doubt. The apparitions, particularly the one about Birnam Wood moving toward Dunsinane, foreshadow Macbeth's demise. When the English forces, led by Malcolm and Macduff, camouflage themselves with branches from Birnam Wood, the prophecy is fulfilled. Macbeth's false sense of invincibility crumbles revealing his vulnerability. His downfall serves as a cautionary tale—a reminder that unchecked ambition corrodes the soul and that eventually rightful leadership transcends mere power.

4. (i) In Ray Bradbury's 'There Will Come Soft Rains', the element of fire serves as a powerful symbol representing both destruction and the indomitable force of nature.

The mechanised house, which is the last remaining structure in a post-apocalyptic world, falls victim to fire. A tree bough crashes through the kitchen window, igniting the whole room. The flames then spread relentlessly, consuming the entire house. Despite the house's advanced technology and fire-repellent systems, it cannot withstand the fire's onslaught. This destruction emphasises on the fragility of human creations when faced with the force of nature.

The mechanised house deploys snake-like tubes to release fire repellent. However, the flames defy these efforts wrapping around the exterior and attacking the attic which apparently is the house's 'brain'. The fire cleverly sends flames outside, shattering the attic's control mechanisms. The house's oak skeleton cringes from the heat, revealing its inner wires and nerves. Despite frantic attempts to extinguish the fire, including automated chores and oblivious announcements, the house succumbs. Hence, this futile struggle to put out the fire shows the overwhelming power of nature rendering even the most advanced technology powerless.

(ii) In the story 'The Medicine Bag', the items within the medicine bag hold profound significance for Martin's family as they bridge generations and cultural heritage.

Grandpa's medicine bag is not merely a physical object as for him; it embodies spiritual power and ancestral wisdom. Passed down through generations, it connects Martin's family to their Sioux heritage and Grandpa's attachment to the bag reflects the belief that it ensures communion between the people and the spirit world.

Martin hesitates to accept the medicine bag because he feels unworthy. His mixed heritage - Sioux and White - creates an internal conflict. He fears disrespecting the sacred bundle by not fully understanding its significance. Martin grapples with his identity, torn between embracing his heritage and fitting into mainstream American culture, which also highlights the struggle of cultural assimilation.

(iii) (a) In the short story 'Atithi', Motilal Babu can be seen as a wealthy landlord who embodies both generosity and curiosity. His benevolence shines through when he encounters Tarapada, the wandering boy. Despite being a stranger, his charismatic appearance captivated Motilal Babu and his family. Their readiness to accept him on their boat reflects their kind nature. Motilal Babu's willingness to share his space and resources with a guest exemplifies traditional Indian hospitality. His generosity extends beyond mere material wealth as he is intrigued by Tarapada's wanderlust and innocence, and wishes to keep him under his care. Rather than dismissing the boy as a mere traveller, Motilal Babu engages in conversation with Tarapada, eager to learn about his family background. His open-mindedness allows him to appreciate the beauty of chance encounters and the richness of human experiences. Therefore, Motilal Babu's decision to welcome Tarapada aboard their boat is multifaceted which shows his humanitarian instinct, adherence to cultural norms and fascination with Tarapada's purity.

Tarapada's innocence and spontaneity cast a spell on everyone in the story, except Charushashi. However, Motilal Babu and Annapurna are still drawn to Tarapada's purity and curiosity as his presence adds an element of intrigue to their journey, breaking the monotony of their routine. Hence, these could be the reasons they took Tarapada in and treated him like their own child.

(b) In Philip K. Dick's short story 'The Cookie Lady', the absence of a specific moral lesson or theme is intentional. Instead, the author masterfully creates an atmosphere of suspense, fear and absurdity. The tale revolves around a chubby boy named Bubber who frequently visits old Mrs. Drew's house for her delicious cookies. Mrs. Drew enjoys Bubber's company and secretly feeds off his youth.

But what Bubber doesn't realise is that she drains his vitality, leaving him weakened and ill after each visit. The story culminates in a shocking revelation which is scary and disturbing as Mrs. Drew transforms into a young, dark-haired beauty while Bubber becomes a mere bundle of trash carried away by the wind.

The story highlights the complexities of human interactions where Mrs. Drew, who seemingly has a kind demeanour, masks her sinister intentions. Bubber's innocent craving for cookies blinds him to the danger lurking beneath the surface and leads him to unwittingly sacrifice his youth. Thus, the tale serves as a cautionary reminder that not all relationships are what they appear to be. The story suggests that unchecked cravings can exact a heavy toll. Mrs. Drew's insatiable hunger for youth mirrors the consequences of uncontrolled or unchecked desire.

To conclude, the story blurs the lines between reality and the inexplicable emphasising the eerie and unsettling aspects of everyday life.

5. (i) In Wole Soyinka's poem 'Telephone Conversation', the speaker's confession, revealing that he is African, elicits a revealing response from the landlady.

When the speaker discloses his ethnicity, the landlady's silence speaks volumes. Her initial pleasant demeanour is replaced by an uncomfortable pause. This silence reflects her underlying prejudice and discomfort upon realising that the potential tenant is black. Despite her outward politeness, her true feelings emerge which is disapproval masked by social decorum.

The speaker cleverly mocks the landlady's ignorance. When she demands to know how 'light' or 'dark' his skin colour is, he responds with a playful twist. He says, 'I am not completely black because my palms and soles are white.' By highlighting this absurdity, he exposes the futility of categorising people based on skin colour, and his reply challenges racial stereotypes and emphasises the shared humanity beyond superficial appearances.

(ii) In Mamang Dai's poem 'Small Towns and the River', vivid imagery weaves together contrasting themes of mortality and eternity. The initial stanzas present a dusty, mournful picture of small towns. The poet laments the frequent news of death that pervades these settlements. The towns become symbols of impermanence where lives subside and ebb away like dust carried by the wind. The imagery of grief and loss in the poem evokes a sense of transience in the readers.

In contrast, the river flows eternally through these towns. It becomes a powerful symbol of continuity and immortality. The river's perpetual movement stands in stark contrast to the fleeting existence of human lives. For the people of the town, the river represents hope, solace and the promise of something enduring beyond mortality.

(iii) (a) John Donne's poem 'Death Be Not Proud' is a powerful meditation on mortality, defiance and the nature of existence. In this poem, Donne personifies death as a proud entity boasting of its power to claim lives. However, the speaker challenges death's arrogance. He asserts that death is not the ultimate victor rather, it is a mere transition, a temporary sleep before awakening to eternal life. The poem celebrates the resilience of the human spirit and the triumph of the soul over physical demise.

The speaker confronts death with courage. He refuses to be intimidated by its supposed might. The repeated refrain 'Death Be Not Proud' emphasises this defiance. The speaker's unwavering resolve suggests that death's dominion is illusory.

The poet infuses the poem with Christian beliefs. He alludes to biblical concepts such as resurrection and eternal life. The phrase 'rest of their bones' implies a peaceful slumber before awakening in the afterlife. The poem echoes the Christian hope of transcending mortality. 'Death Be Not Proud' encourages readers to reevaluate their fear of death. It suggests that death is merely a passage—a momentary interruption—before the soul's eternal journey. The poem's defiant tone invites us to embrace life fully knowing that death's sting is temporary. Ultimately, it celebrates the resilience of the human spirit and the hope of something beyond the grave.

(b) In Shane Koyczan's poem 'Beethoven', the relationship between Ludwig van Beethoven and his father is portrayed as tumultuous and is marked by abuse.

Beethoven's father habitually mistreated him and the poem suggests that he was not only verbally harsh but also physically violent. The line 'his father made a habit out of hitting him' reveals the severity of the abuse. This mistreatment likely left lasting scars on Beethoven's psyche. His father held high expectations for his son. The poem implies that he wanted Beethoven to become a genius—a musical prodigy. However, this desire for greatness came at a steep cost. His father's relentless pressure and criticism likely fueled the young composer's determination and additionally contributed to his emotional struggles.

Beethoven's upbringing in a house where 'a name meant nothing' suggests a lack of familiar warmth or connection. His father's harshness isolated him emotionally. Despite his talent and passion for music, Beethoven faced rejection and hardship within his own family.

In conclusion, Beethoven's relationship with his father was fraught with abuse, unattainable expectations and emotional isolation. These experiences likely shaped Beethoven's resilience and determination but they also left scars that influenced his music and personal life where music was his only way of expression.

SQP Code : **PB-8/10** | Series ***i*-Succeed 8-25/10** | Roll No.

Sample Question Paper 08

Literature in English 12th (Code 801)

General Instructions

1. It has 5 questions in all.
2. Answer all questions.
3. While answering Question 1 in Section A, you are required to write only ONE option as the correct answer.
4. Internal choice has been given in the long answer questions on Drama, Prose and Poetry.
5. Do not exceed the prescribed word limit while answering the questions in Section B.
6. The intended marks for questions are given in brackets [ ].

Time : 3 Hrs.

Max. Marks : 80

Section A (20 Marks)

Question 1.

Choose the correct option for the following questions. (10)

(i) Who is the speaker of the following lines according to Act IV of the play *Macbeth*? [Recall]

'…His flight was madness. When our actions do not,
Our fears do make us traitors….'

(a) Banquo (b) The witches
(c) Lady Macbeth (d) Lady Macduff

(ii) In Act III of the play *Macbeth*, why does Macbeth throw a fit and behave irrationally at his own banquet? [Analysis]

(a) As he is gone crazy with power (b) Due to his servant's mistake
(c) Due to Lady Macbeth's behaviour (d) He sees Banquo's ghost

(iii) In the following lines in Act V of the play, what does the speaker mean? [Understanding]

'Here's the smell of the blood still. All the perfumes of Arabia will not sweeten this little hand.'

(a) Nothing can hide the truth of their crimes
(b) The perfume she has is not strong enough
(c) She smells blood in the room
(d) She does not like the perfumes from Arabia

(iv) Based on your reading of Acts IV, which of the following statements from the play reflects the tone of the conversation between Macduff and Malcolm? [Analysis]

(P) They are honest towards each other
(Q) They are melancholic
(R) They exhibit anger towards Banquo
(S) They are diplomatic

(a) (P) and (Q)
(b) (Q) and (S)
(c) (P) (R) and (S)
(d) (Q) and (R)

(v) Why did Motilal Babu move the boat near the riverside market in the story 'Atithi'? [Understanding]

(a) To buy groceries
(b) To get fresh meal prepared
(c) To get some clothes
(d) To buy books

(vi) Based on the story 'There Will Come Soft Rains', how are the following statements related? [Analysis]

Statement I 'The five spots of paint remained...'

Statement II 'At night the city gave off a radioactive glow...'

(a) Statement I and II are the same.
(b) Statement I is a result of Statement II.
(c) Statement I and II are unrelated.
(d) Statement II is a result of statement I.

(vii) Who is the main character in the story 'Indigo'? [Recall]

(a) Tarapada
(b) Charushashi
(c) Sukhanram
(d) Aniruddha

(viii) The poem 'Tithonus' was written by [Recall]

(a) Alfred, Lord Tennyson.
(b) John Donne.
(c) William Wordsworth.
(d) Mamang Dai.

(ix) In the poem 'Telephone Conversation', what is the conversation about? [Understanding]

(a) Pizza order
(b) Renting a house
(c) Customer service
(d) Job interview

(x) In the poem 'Beethoven', what is Beethoven's source of inspiration? [Interpret]

(a) His friends
(b) His family
(c) His sufferings
(d) His teacher

Question 2.

Complete the following sentences by providing a reason for each in brief. Do not write the question. (10)

(i) In Act IV of the play *Macbeth*, Malcolm does not immediately believe Macduff's intentions because .... [Analysis]

(ii) In Act III of the play, Lady Macbeth had to send all the guests away because .... [Recall]

(iii) In Act III, Macbeth tells the murderers 'Thou art the best o' the cut-throats' because .... [Understanding]

(iv) Macbeth was confident that Malcolm couldn't defeat him because .... [Interpret]

(v) Tarapada ran away from home at a very young age because .... [Recall]

(vi) Bubber could not see the changes in Mrs. Drew's appearance because .... [Analysis]

(vii) In the story 'There Will Come Soft Rains', the city appeared to have a radioactive glow because .... [Understanding]

(viii) In the poem 'Small Towns and the River', the poet's tone is sad because .... [Understanding]

(ix) Beethoven's father hit him because .... [Recall]

(x) In the poem 'Death Be Not Proud', the speaker is not afraid of death because .... [Analysis]

Section B *(60 Marks)*

Macbeth-William Shakespeare

Question 3.

(i) Briefly discuss the conversation between Macbeth and Lady Macbeth before the banquet in Act III Scene 2 of the play. Give your answer in 100-150 words incorporating the following details [Understanding] (5)

(a) The tone of the conversation (b) Macbeth being upset

(ii) In Act IV, why do the witches summon the apparitions? Give your answer in 100-150 words incorporating the following details [Analysis] (5)

(a) Nature of the apparitions

(b) Macbeth's reaction to the apparitions

(iii) (a) With appropriate examples from the play, discuss the importance of Lady Macduff's character in the play *Macbeth*. Write your answer in 200-250 words. [Evaluate] (10)

Or

(b) How does Lady Macbeth's role contribute to Macbeth's downfall? Discuss in 200-250 words. [Evaluate]

Prism-A Collection of Short Stories

Question 4.

(i) Describe Tarapada and Motilal Babu's meeting from the story 'Atithi'. Write your answer in 100-150 words incorporating the following details. [Evaluate] (5)

(a) Tarapada's request

(b) Motilal Babu accepting Tarapada's request

(ii) Based on the story 'The Cookie Lady', describe Mrs. Drew. Write your answer in 100-150 words incorporating the following details. [Understanding] (5)

(a) She lured Bubber into her house (b) Her intentions with Bubber

(iii) (a) How do you think the house in the story 'There Will Come Soft Rains' is a replica of the natural world? Discuss in 200-250 words. [Analysis] (10)

Or

(b) Based on your reading of the story 'The Medicine Bag', comment on Martin's character in 200-250 words. [Evaluate]

SP-08

Rhapsody-Poetry

Question 5.

(i) Discuss briefly the meaning and impact of the opening lines of the poem 'Death Be Not Proud' in 100-150 words incorporating the following details. [Understanding] (5)

(a) The powerlessness of death

(b) Death not 'killing' a person

(ii) Beethoven grew up listening to his father's 'anthem' of 'not good enough'. Evaluate the statement and write your answer in 100-150 words incorporating the following details: [Evaluate] (5)

(a) The effect of this on Beethoven's psyche

(b) Beethoven's habit to never praise anyone

(iii) (a) In the poem 'Telephone Conversation' by Wole Soyinka, what social issue has been addressed? Evaluate in 200-250 words. [Recall] (10)

Or

(b) In reference to the lines "Release me, and restore me to the ground. Thou seest all things, thou wilt see my grave", from the poem 'Tithonus', elaborate on what 'all things' does Aurora see in 200-250 words. [Evaluate]

Answers *in Topper's Style*

1. (i) (d) Lady Macduff
(ii) (d) He sees Banquo's ghost
(iii) (a) Nothing can hide the truth
(iv) (b) (Q) and (S)
(v) (b) To get fresh meal prepared
(vi) (a) Statement I and II are the same.
(vii) (d) Aniruddha
(viii) (a) Alfred, Lord Tennyson.
(ix) (b) Renting a house
(x) (c) His sufferings

2. (i) he fears that Macduff has been sent by Macbeth as an agent to destroy Malcolm's efforts
(ii) Macbeth couldn't handle his emotions, and he started getting loud and aggressive as he kept seeing Banquo's ghost everywhere
(iii) he is impressed by the murderers when they tell him they have cut Banquo's throat
(iv) as per the second apparition, 'no man born of woman' could kill him
(v) he had a deep longing for exploring the world and couldn't be tied in any kind of bonds, even the bonds of family
(vi) he was too focused on the cookies to notice his surroundings
(vii) the city had been destroyed by the nuclear explosion and the radioactive gases from it glowed at night
(viii) the poem discusses the deep effect of the death of a person on lives of people in the small towns
(ix) he was frustrated and wanted Beethoven to turn out a genius
(x) according to him, it holds no power and is as temporary as resting or sleeping

3. (i) In Act III Scene 2, Macbeth and Lady Macbeth can be seen sharing their unhappiness with each other before the night of the banquet. This short conversation between the murderous couple helps the readers get an insight on their inner thoughts. Lady Macbeth tries to soothe her husband through encouraging words but she herself has the same doubts as him. Killing Duncan invited more troubles for them than they had imagined. The tone of this conversation is of anxiety and unease as both Macbeth and Lady Macbeth share their inner turmoil. Lady Macbeth advises Macbeth to conceal his distress during the banquet urging him to be cheerful among their guests. Macbeth, however, expresses bitterness and fear. He is upset because Banquo and his son, Fleance pose a threat to his reign.

(ii) In Act IV Scene 1, the witches summon the apparitions as Macbeth commands them to. Macbeth, due to his paranoia about losing the throne that he had acquired through his dark deeds, wished to know more about his fate. The apparitions, just like the witches, are eerie and horrifying. The first apparition is an armed head warning Macbeth to beware Macduff; the second, a bloody child, reassures him that no man born of woman can harm him; and, lastly, a child crowned with a tree tells Macbeth he won't be overthrown until Birnam Wood moves to Dunsinane. Initially, Macbeth becomes confident as he learns this new information but soon it vanishes as the witches say 'Ay sir, all this is so'. There can be no equivocation, no argument with Fate and he needs to accept what he had just seen.

(iii) (a) Lady Macduff's character in the play *Macbeth* is a small but important one. She plays a crucial role in highlighting themes and stands in contrast to Lady Macbeth. Her innocence and vulnerability stand in stark contrast to the ruthless ambition of the other characters in the play. Lady Macduff shows maternal love and devotion as, when she learns of her husband's flight to England, she worries about her and her child's safety whereas Lady Macbeth does not think of anything in order to accomplish her ambitions.

Lady Macduff also serves as a foil to Lady Macbeth's character. While Lady Macbeth manipulates her husband into committing Duncan's murder, Lady Macduff remains loyal and honest to her values. Her condemnation of Macduff's absence highlights the contrast between the two women. She lacks cunning and deceit.

Furthermore, Lady Macduff and her family are victims of Macbeth's tyranny. Their brutal murder by Macbeth's hired murderers underscores the play's theme of unchecked ambition leading to violence and destruction. Lady Macduff's death serves as an important reminder of the consequences of political upheaval. This event also highlights the atmosphere of chaos and brutality in Macbeth's reign as he goes on to mercilessly kill anyone that appears a threat to him.

(b) In the play *Macbeth*, Lady Macbeth plays an important role in Macbeth's downfall. She acts as a catalyst by provoking him to pursue the throne. She manipulates Macbeth into murdering Duncan by challenging his manliness. She plants the seed of ambition in Macbeth's consciousness which ultimately contributes to his downfall. Even when Macbeth gets upset and regrets his actions, she steps in to justify them and further manipulates him.

After Duncan's murder, Lady Macbeth initially remains resolute but soon her conscience begins to torment her. She sleepwalks trying to wash imaginary bloodstains from her hands. Her guilt and deteriorating mental state mirror Macbeth's own descent into madness. Their shared guilt binds them together but it also unravels their sanity. As a result, Macbeth, after his acquisition of the throne, becomes distant and secretive which makes him lonelier and devoid of any emotional support. This transition in Lady Macbeth and Macbeth's relationship makes him even more reliant on the witches' prophecies.

An example of Macbeth's deteriorating psyche can be drawn from the banquet scene. During the banquet, Lady Macbeth tries to maintain appearances urging Macbeth to hide his inner turmoil. However, his hallucination of Banquo's ghost reveals his guilt and paranoia. Lady Macbeth's inability to control the situation further destabilises Macbeth.

4. (i) Tarapada first meets Motilal Babu while looking for a way to get to Nandigram village. Motilal Babu was travelling to Kathaliya village by his boat along with his wife, Annapurna and daughter, Charushashi. On seeing Tarapada's charming appearance and attitude, Motilal Babu and Annapurna made acquaintance with him and accepted him as a guest on his boat. Under the spell of Tarapada's charismatic presence, Motilal Babu agreed to give him a lift to Nandigram when he asked. He couldn't say no to Tarapada as he was just a boy away from home and was very innocent and, from his looks, Motilal Babu judged that he belonged to a good family too. However, later on, Tarapada stayed with Motilal Babu's family for a while.

(ii) As per the story 'The Cookie Lady', Mrs. Drew was an elderly lady who lived alone in her house. Although she had an eerie presence about her and was known as the 'creepy old lady' in the neighbourhood, her demeanour around Bubber appeared to be kind and warm.

Mrs. Drew lured Bubber into her house by baking fresh cookies and offering them to Bubber when he passed by her house. Bubber, being a child, loved cookies and easily fell into Mrs. Drew's trap. She would bake him fresh cookies each day and ask him to read to spend more time in his company. Her intentions although were evil as, whenever Bubber sat near Mrs. Drew, reading out from his school books, she began to change supernaturally into a beautiful young woman. Eventually, she sucked all of Bubber's vitality and youth when he informed her that he wouldn't be visiting her anymore.

(iii) (a) In Ray Bradbury's 'There Will Come Soft Rains', the house serves as a striking yet eerie representation of the natural world. Despite being an artificially intelligent, automated machine, the house attempts to mimic the rhythms and routines of nature.

The house replicates daily activities such as waking the family, preparing breakfast and maintaining cleanliness. Its voice-clock even mimics the urgency of nature urging inhabitants to rise at seven o'clock. Other imitations of natural elements that were present in the house were the robotic mice who cleaned it, the aluminium roaches and the iron crickets. Also, the artificial animals in the nursery depict the beauty of wildlife inside the house.

Although the house was able to withstand the nuclear explosion, it couldn't stand against the power of nature. The falling of a tree branch, due to wind, caused the house to catch fire and then the house's futile efforts to put out the fire show nature's ultimate power and the limitations of human technology.

The house also embodies negative traits associated with technology such as obsession with control, order and insensitivity. This story should be taken as a cautionary tale against our blind reliance on technology in today's world and the limitations of technology.

(b) In the story 'The Medicine Bag', Martin is the central character. He is a young boy living in the city of Iowa with his family. Martin's character develops from being embarrassed of his Grandpa's appearance that does not match the popular standards and the image of Indians on the tv to embracing his heritage and culture wholeheartedly.

Like many kids his age, Martin prioritises popularity and social acceptance from his peers. He avoids anything that might disrupt his carefully curated image. Initially, he resents his grandfather's presence fearing that it will interfere with his modern city-identity. Martin's reluctance to acknowledge his heritage mirrors the generational conflict between tradition and contemporary life.

However, as the story progresses, we see Martin slowly embracing his culture, and his hesitation and fear of his friends meeting his Grandpa vanishing. Martin initially avoids his friends from coming to visit his grandfather but, one day, when they follow him home, Grandpa puts on his best beaded vest and his favourite moccasins. Martin feels ashamed of his own feelings as his friends are impressed by Grandpa and do not laugh at him for being exotic like he had envisioned. Later on, when Grandpa explains the history and significance of the medicine bag to him, he feels proud of his roots. Ultimately, Martin accepts his mixed identity with love and respect. After his grandfather's passing, he wears the medicine bag symbolising his connection to his culture and his ancestors. The boastful boy, Martin, through the course of the story turns into a thoughtful and proud person.

5. (i) According to the opening lines of John Donne's 'Death Be Not Proud', death should not be proud of itself as it is scary and terrifying to some people. In these lines, the speaker directly addresses death personifying it as a living entity. By challenging the conventional perception of death as an all-powerful, fearsome force, the poet asserts that death is not to be feared. He clearly declares that death does not kill people and it cannot kill him as our souls are eternal beings. According to the poet, death holds no power and is merely a 'deep sleep'. It cannot 'kill' people as, when it comes, our souls move to another dimension and we continue our spiritual journeys.

(ii) Beethoven had a rough childhood and faced tumultuous upbringing due to his father's drinking and abusing habits. The constant bullying and harsh treatment left a lasting impact on his psyche. Whenever Beethoven attempted to play the piano, his father's voice echoed in his mind declaring his efforts as 'not good enough'. These words became a perpetual anthem, haunting him even as he composed symphonies that enthralled audiences. His incurable deafness added to his struggles yet he persevered with unwavering determination. No matter how good he played, his father was never satisfied which eventually made Beethoven never appreciate anyone despite achieving perfection and popularity. In a way, this reflects his own pursuit of perfection.

(iii) (a) Wole Soyinka's poem 'Telephone Conversation' accurately addresses the pervasive social issue of racial discrimination. Through a seemingly mundane telephone call, Soyinka exposes the absurdity and hypocrisy of prejudice. In the poem, the speaker, an African man, engages in a conversation with a lady regarding renting an apartment. The landlady's advertisement for the apartment claims that race is not a problem for her.

However, when the black man reveals his identity, her attitude immediately changes. She hesitates but asks him anyway about the colour of his skin to which the speaker very cleverly replies. Without giving her a direct answer, he starts giving her absurd responses which eventually embarrass her and she refuses to engage further. The landlady's question to the speaker reveals her hypocrisy and racial bias. The poet has masterfully employed irony and satire in the poem as he highlights the landlady's polite veneer contrasted sharply with her offensive questions. The poem exposes the incongruity between the landlady's 'good-breeding' and her discriminatory behaviour. While the poem specifically addresses racial bias, its themes resonate universally. It reminds us that prejudice can infiltrate even mundane interactions. This poem shows how, in supposed neutral spaces, discrimination and racial biases still linger and affect people deeply.

(b) Tennyson's poem relates the myth of Tithonus a mortal man who loved by Aurora, the goddess of the dawn. He was exceedingly beautiful and, when she fell in love with him, she took him from the mortal realm to live in her palace in the East. In the early stages of their relationship, Tithonus asked for a gift from the goddess-immortality so that he could be with her forever. And, though he received this gift, he could not be happy with her for long because Aurora neglected to grant him eternal youth. Tithonus is now condemned to age forever, far beyond the capabilities of the human body.

When the poem states that she "seest all thing", it is referring to the fact that Aurora is an all-knowing goddess. The gods and goddesses have knowledge of much more than what mere mortals do so she was able to see all things. They are omnipresent and omniscient and, thus, can also predict things that have not happened yet. Furthermore, as the goddess of dawn, she opened up each day bringing sunlight to the entire Earth. This shows her wisdom and is a way in which she sees all things.

In the last stanza of the poem, Tithonus is pleading with Aurora to just let him die. He just wants life to end, to leave his aged and frail body behind and find rest in the Earth. Thus, he says that, if she grants his wish and takes away his immortality, she will see his dead body just like she sees everything else. According to him, she would not have to suffer through something new.

SQP Code : **PB-9/10** Series ***i*-Succeed 9-25/10** Roll No. | | | | | | | | |

Sample Question Paper 09

Literature in English 12th (Code 801)

General Instructions

1. It has 5 questions in all.
2. Answer all questions.
3. While answering Question 1 in Section A, you are required to write only ONE option as the correct answer.
4. Internal choice has been given in the long answer questions on Drama, Prose and Poetry.
5. Do not exceed the prescribed word limit while answering the questions in Section B.
6. The intended marks for questions are given in brackets [ ].

Time : 3 Hrs.

Max. Marks : 80

Section A (20 Marks)

Question 1.

Choose the correct option for the following questions. (10)

(i) Who is the speaker of the following lines according to Act IV of the play *Macbeth*? [Recall]

"...I pray you school yourself. But for your husband,
He is noble, wise, judicious, and best knows
The fits o' th' season. I dare not speak much..."

(a) Lady Macduff (b) The witches
(c) Lady Macbeth (d) Ross

(ii) Who arrives with the troops before the Dunsinane Castle? [Recall]

(a) Menteith (b) Malcolm (c) Macduff (d) Fleance

(iii) In Act III of the play, what is the tone of Lennox's comments about Macbeth? [Understanding]

(a) Sarcastic (b) Respectful (c) Hateful (d) Aggressive

(iv) In Act IV of the play *Macbeth*, why does Malcolm doubt Macduff? [Analysis]

(P) As he thinks he works for Macbeth
(Q) As he has personal issues with him
(R) As he doesn't trust him
(S) As he is afraid of him

(a) (P) and (Q) (b) (P) and (R)
(c) (Q) and (R) (d) (S) and (Q)

(v) Where did Tarapada intend to go by boat in the story 'Atithi'? [Recall]

(a) Kolkata (b) Nandigram
(c) Kathaliya (d) Dumka

(vi) Based on your reading of 'There Will Come Soft Rains', select the correct option. [Analysis]

Statement I But no doors slammed, no carpets took the soft tread of rubber heels.

Statement II And the rain tapped on the empty house, echoing.

(a) Statement I and II are the same.
(b) Statement I is a result of Statement II.
(c) Statement I and II are unrelated.
(d) Statement II is a result of statement I.

(vii) Why did the truck driver keep honking at Aniruddha in the story 'Indigo'? [Analysis]

(a) Because he was driving in the wrong lane (b) Because the car was blocking the road
(c) Because he wanted to warn Aniruddha (d) None of these

(viii) Who wrote the poem 'Small Towns and the River'? [Recall]

(a) Wole Soyinka (b) Mamang Dai
(c) Shane Koyczan (d) John Donne

(ix) In the poem 'Death Be Not Proud', what is the main theme? [Understanding]

(a) Immortality (b) Transience of human life
(c) Romance (d) Impotency of death

(x) In the poem 'Beethoven', which musical instrument holds significance? [Recall]

(a) Drums (b) Piccolo (c) Piano (d) Flute

Question 2.

Complete the following sentences by providing a reason for each in brief. Do not write the question. (10)

(i) During the banquet in Act III, Macbeth says he will mingle with the society first and not Lady Macbeth because .... [Understanding]

(ii) The witches were asked to meet at the pit of Acheron because .... [Recall]

(iii) In Act V, the doctor reveals that he wished he was away from Dunsinane because .... [Understanding]

(iv) Fleance is compared to a "dangerous worm" by Macbeth because .... [Analysis]

(v) During his travels, Tarapada joined a group of singers because .... [Recall]

(vi) In the story 'The Cookie Lady', Mrs. Drew wanted Bubber to read to her because .... [Understanding]

(vii) In the story 'Indigo', Aniruddha's neighbour was worried about him because .... [Recall]

(viii) Tithonus is granted the gift of immortality because .... [Recall]

(ix) In the poem 'Telephone Conversation', the speaker does not give a direct answer to the landlady because .... [Analysis]

(x) In the poem 'Death Be Not Proud', there is irony because .... [Understanding]

Section B (60 Marks)

Macbeth-William Shakespeare

Question 3.

(i) In Act III Scene 4, why does Lady Macbeth send all the guests away? [Analysis] (5)
 (a) The change in Macbeth's behaviour
 (b) The atmosphere of the event

(ii) In Act III, Macbeth tells the murderers "Thou art the best o' the cut-throats". Why does he say that? [Analysis] (5)
 (a) What does it say about Macbeth?
 (b) The details of the statement gives about the murderers

(iii) (a) Discuss the character of Lennox based on the acts prescribed your answer write in 200-250 words. [Understanding] (10)

Or

 (b) Why was Macbeth convinced that he was invincible over Macduff's army? Discuss Macbeth's downfall and his character traits that enabled it in 200-250 words. [Evaluate]

Prism-A Collection of Short Stories

Question 4.

(i) Briefly describe Tarapada's journey to Kathaliya on Motilal Babu's boat from the story 'Atithi'. Write your answer in 100-150 words including the following details. [Evalaute] (5)
 (a) Development of a bond between Tarapada and the family
 (b) Charushashi's behaviour towards Tarapada

(ii) What was the reaction of Bubber's parents when they saw Bubber exhausted after meeting Mrs. Drew? Write your answer in 100-150 words based on the story 'The Cookie Lady' incorporating the following details. [Recall] (5)
 (a) The action that Bubber's parents took
 (b) Did it stop Bubber from visiting Mrs. Drew?

SP-09

(iii) (a) Why was Anirrudha, in the short story 'Indigo', unable to act as per his wish even though he was fully conscious of his body? Discuss in 200-250 words. [Analysis] (10)

Or

 (b) Describe the commotion in the street on Grandpa's arrival based on your reading of the story 'The Medicine Bag'. Write your answer in 200-250 words. [Understanding]

Rhapsody-Poetry

Question 5.

(i) State the significance and theme in the line "The woods decay, the woods decay and fall" in the poem 'Tithonus'. Give your answer in 100-150 words incorporating the following details. [Evaluate] (5)
 (a) What do we infer about the speaker?
 (b) The speaker's relation to the natural world

(ii) Comment on the repeated line, "Life and death...only the rituals are permanent" in the poem 'Small Towns and the River'. Give your answer in 100-150 words incorporating the following details. [Evaluate] (5)

(a) The repetition of this line

(b) The theme emphasised

(iii) (a) Comment on the impact of pain and suffering on Beethoven's music. Give your answer in 200-250 words. [Analysis] (10)

Or

(b) With the reference to the poem 'Telephone Conversation', discuss how the speaker's tone changes as the lady enquires about his skin colour. Give your answer in 200-250 words. [Evaluate]

Answers *in Topper's Style*

1. (i) (d) Ross
   (ii) (b) Malcolm
   (iii) (a) sarcastic
   (iv) (b) (P) and (R)
   (v) (b) Nandigram
   (vi) (a) Statement I and II are the same.
   (vii) (b) Because the car was blocking the road
   (viii) (b) Mamang Dai
   (ix) (d) Impotency of death
   (x) (c) Piano

2. (i) Lady Macbeth was to acquire the throne for sometime and she would welcome the guests formally when the time was right
   (ii) there they were going to meet Macbeth and trick him to his destruction
   (iii) he was upset with the general unrest and other things that were happening in and around the castle; for example, the preparation for war and Lady Macbeth's condition
   (iv) he fears that, just like a small serpent grows fangs when it grows up, Fleance too might become a threat for him after a while
   (v) of his passion for music
   (vi) she wanted to spend more time in his presence to feel younger and rejuvenated
   (vii) it was nighttime and Aniruddha hadn't hired a driver for his 200-mile drive
   (viii) his lover, Aurora (or Eos) is a goddess and, when he expresses his love to her, she grants him the gift
   (ix) he's taken aback by the absurdity of her question about his skin colour and expresses his anger and frustration in a creative way by not giving her a direct answer
   (x) even though the poet writes that he's not afraid of death, he still can't avert it's inevitable arrival

3. (i) In Act III Scene 4 of the play, Lady Macbeth sends all the guests away due to Macbeth's aggressive reactions to the sighting of Banquo's ghost which only he could see. As the banquet begins, Macbeth is informed of Banquo's death and Fleance's escape by one of Banquo's murderers. The impact of this news is such that Macbeth starts hallucinating and seeing Banquo's ghost sitting on the throne. Lady Macbeth tries to avert the guests' attention by dismissing Macbeth's behaviour as a temporary fit but, when the ghost reappears, she realises the severity of the situation and sends everyone away.

   At the beginning of the banquet, the atmosphere is that of joy and celebration. However, the appearance of Banquo's ghost and Macbeth's erratic behaviour creates tension and fear. Therefore, Lady Macbeth's decision to send the guests away reflects her innate fear of the truth of their dark deeds being revealed.

   (ii) In Act III, Macbeth says "Thou art the best o' the cut-throats" when the murderers tell him that they've cut Banquo's throat. He says so because he is impressed by their efficiency. The phrase "best o' the cut-throats" suggests that these murderers are highly proficient at their trade. They are skilled executioners, adept at carrying out deadly deeds. Macbeth's praise of the murderers and their efficiency shows the dark side of his nature. First, he values them as tools to conduct his dark deeds; and second, his choice of words for praising and expressing admiration for such a task, that is killing his friend Banquo, shows his truly evil nature. His willingness to employ such ruthless individuals highlights his descent into darkness. Macbeth, once noble, now embraces treachery and bloodshed.

(iii) (a) Lennox is a young nobleman attending on Macbeth in the play. He plays a small yet significant role in the play as he works in close proximity to Macbeth. Lennox can be seen as an observant and sceptical man. With his keen eye, he gets to know of Macbeth's ambition and deception early on in the play. In Act III, he suspects that Macbeth has been involved in the murder of King Duncan and he even doubts Macbeth when he kills Duncan's guards. His key moment occurs in the play when he tries to expose Macbeth's guilt and deception to like-minded lords by using ironic phrases during their conversations about Duncan's murder. His scepticism hints at the unravelling of Macbeth's rule. However, despite his doubts and scepticism, Lennox stays with Macbeth till the end, but, when Malcolm attacks Dunsinane, Lennox deserts Macbeth to join Malcolm and Macduff.

In conclusion, Lennox can be seen as a character who was loyal not to Macbeth but to his own country. Lennox's transformation from a loyal observer to a critical thinker underscores the pervasive fear and unease in Scotland under Macbeth's rule. His character adds depth to the play by providing an alternative perspective to the events, and his observations and comments serve as a contrast to the actions of Macbeth and Lady Macbeth highlighting their immoral and destructive behaviour.

(b) Macbeth was blinded with power and ambition in his pursuit of securing the throne for himself. To fuel this fire, Lady Macbeth had provoked him and the apparitions shown by the witches had further made him think he was invincible. As per the apparitions, Macbeth couldn't be defeated by any man born of woman or till the Birnam forest started moving. Due to these prophecies, Macbeth thought he couldn't be defeated by Macduff's army in any way.

Macbeth's character goes through a massive change throughout the play. The seed of ambition planted in his consciousness by Lady Macbeth and the witches, grows and consumes his entire being. When he hears of the possibility of acquiring the throne one day and shares it with Lady Macbeth, she urges him to act fast and grab the opportunity presented to them even if that meant killing the King Duncan. After Duncan's murder, Macbeth assumes the throne but he still isn't satisfied as he fears that the witches' other prophecies may also come true and Banquo's son may take his crown so he decides to remove them from his way.

In this way, his constant fear and paranoia consumes him and he makes impulsive decisions one after the other pushing himself into the depth of darkness, ultimately leading to his downfall.

4. (i) Tarapada's boat journey to Kathaliya was interesting and memorable. As their boat sailed through shimmering waters, Tarapada thoroughly enjoyed the beautiful sceneries they came across and formed a beautiful bond with Motilal Babu and Annapurna. He helped with the chores and even entertained them with his acting and singing skills. He cast a spell of his innocence on Motilal Babu and Annapurna, and they both cherished his presence in their lives. However, for the same reasons, Charushashi developed jealousy towards Tarapada as she was a single child and did not like sharing her parents' affections. Therefore, she never left a chance to express her anger towards Tarapada. She cried and made excuses to get her parents' attention whenever she saw them enjoying Tarapada's company or praising him for his talents.

(ii) Bubber's parents were upset with him when he returned home late from Mrs. Drew's house. Annoyed that he disobeyed their instructions not to stay out too long and not to go to a stranger's house, they expressed their concern about his exhaustion and the strange influence Mrs. Drew seemed to have on him. Bubber's father had a bad feeling about Mrs. Drew; therefore, he forbade Bubber from visiting her again but, when Bubber insisted that he wished to see her one last time and say goodbye, his mother agreed. Hence, Bubber went to Mrs. Drew's house for one last time so that he could have all the cookies he wanted and tell her that he will not be returning as per his parents' instructions. Therefore, his parents' warning couldn't stop Bubber from visiting Mrs. Drew or from becoming her prey.

(iii) (a) During his night stay at the Dak Bungalow, Aniruddha has a strange and almost supernatural experience. As per the story 'Indigo', the protagonist, Aniruddha wakes up in the middle of the night by a scratching noise on his door and, when he moves to inspect the sounds, he realises that, although he is conscious of his body and his surroundings, he is unable to control his actions. When he pays attention to his own hands and appearance of the rest of the body, he further realises that he has been transformed into an Englishman from the time of British rule in India and even his surroundings had change. To his horror, he started moving in the direction he didn't intend to and started writing in a diary that appeared to be the Englishman's journal.

Soon, he was in a shock when he read the words written and realised it was a suicide note. Anirrudha was horrified and overwhelmed with this whole phenomenon which he did not have any control on and, as soon as he finished writing, the man took out a gun and shot his dog, and then put it on his own forehead. Aniruddha felt the horror deeply and was surprised to find everything go back to normal when he woke up. This whole experience made Aniruddha doubt himself and feel as if he was possessed by the spirit of the Englishman; moreover, on his 100th death anniversary.

(b) In the short story 'The Medicine Bag', the arrival of Grandpa stirs up quite a scene in the neighbourhood. The Sun hangs low in the sky casting long shadows across the dusty street. As Grandpa walks down the sidewalk, his attire defies convention, his fringed leather jacket, beaded vest and a feather tucked behind one ear makes him appear as if he were from a different world. The neighbourhood dogs, usually indifferent to passersby, bark in protest as they sense the strangeness about this visitor.

Martin freezes and squirms in embarrassment as he recognises the cause of this commotion and the strange visitor to be his Grandpa. However, he instantly feels a regret for his feelings of embarrassment when he sees his sister Cheryl and his mother happily welcoming him.

The cause of Martin's embarrassment is rooted in the boastful stories that he had told his friends about his Grandpa. As per his stories, Grandpa looked like the tall and strong Indians as shown on TV. Therefore, he felt a jolt of shock when he saw that Grandpa had come to Iowa unannounced and now his friends will be able to see him for who he really is, and may make fun of him and his culture.

In a way, the commotion in the street also represents the stirring up of emotions that Martin felt when he saw his Grandpa.

5. (i) In the poem 'Tithonus', the line "The woods decay, the woods decay and fall" holds profound thematic significance. Tithonus, the speaker, is a mortal who was granted immortality by the goddess Aurora (Eos). However, this gift soon became a curse for Tithonus. Unlike the natural world which ages, decays and eventually renews itself, Tithonus remains frozen in perpetual existence. The repetition of 'decay' in the poem shows the relentless passage of time for everything around, except him.

He yearns for release longing to return to the earth's natural cycle of life and death. Tithonus' relationship with nature is one of envy and sorrow as he witnesses the beauty of renewal in the woods and the swan, yet he himself is denied this natural rhythm. His immortality becomes a burden and a curse, and he laments his inability to share in the organic processes that define human existence.

(ii) In Mamang Dai's poem 'Small Towns and the River', the repeated line "Life and death...only the rituals are permanent" serves as a sad reflection on mortality and the enduring nature of rituals. It serves as a powerful literary device contributing significantly to the central theme of the poem. This line marks the extreme differences between human lives and the cyclic nature of the rituals they practise. These rituals, whether relating to birth, marriage or funeral rites, provide structure and continuity even as lives ebb away. The repetition reinforces the idea that rituals endure beyond individual lives connecting generations and preserving cultural practices. Rituals in our lives whether lighting lamps, chanting prayers or performing last rites have become our bedrock. They outlast individuals binding our communities together. The line underscores the importance of these customs in navigating life's uncertainties.

(iii) (a) Shane Koyczan's poem 'Beethoven' delves into the profound theme of love using vivid imagery and emotional resonance. It discusses how Beethoven dealt with pain through his creativity. Beethoven, the iconic composer, suffered both physically and emotionally, unable to find love within the confines of his home. His father's abusive behaviour left scars that ran deep, making it challenging for him to connect with others. Therefore, he sought solace in his music—a refuge where he could express the inexpressible. Despite his deafness, he transformed emotion into symphonies creating a language that transcended mere notes. Koyczan's portrayal emphasises that to truly understand Beethoven, one must listen to his compositions, for they reveal the depths of his soul and the universal power of love.

The statement "Beethoven's pain and suffering translates into music, and music becomes his creative outlet" encapsulates the profound connection between the composer's emotional turmoil and his artistic expression. He grappled with other personal challenges too, such as hearing loss, unrequited love and societal upheaval. His compositions, particularly during his middle and late periods, bear witness to this inner struggle. They serve as a testament to the transformative power of art where pain finds solace and creativity becomes a beacon of hope.

(b) In Wole Soyinka's poem 'Telephone Conversation', the speaker's tone undergoes a significant shift when the lady enquires about his skin colour. Initially, the speaker encounters silence in response to stereotypical questions about his skin colour reflecting the racism prevalent at the time. As the lady presses further demanding to know if the speaker is 'light' or 'dark,' his tone becomes more defensive and sarcastic. Her questions expose her hypocrisy and her discrimination and the speaker's silence shows how her words shock and confuse him as he cannot believe that such absurd things actually happen to people. However, the speaker cleverly handles the situation and responds by comparing his skin colour to 'sepia' and then to a mix of brunette and blonde, highlighting the absurdity of reducing human identity to simplistic categories and giving the landlady a taste of her own medicine. The lady's inquiry affects the speaker because it exposes her racial bias against him, forcing the speaker to navigate this discriminatory conversation. Thus, the poem highlights the casual racism that people of colour often encounter, emphasising the importance of addressing such biases in society.

The speaker doesn't only call out the landlady's blunt racism but also criticises the way she thinks about the human race itself. By doing this, the speaker refuses to let the complexity of human identity be reduced by the ignorant choice that the landlady offers.

SQP Code : **PB-10/10**

Series ***i*-Succeed 10-25/10**

Roll No.

Sample Question Paper 10

Literature in English 12th (Code 801)

General Instructions

1. It has 5 questions in all.
2. Answer all questions.
3. While answering Question 1 in Section A, you are required to write only ONE option as the correct answer.
4. Internal choice has been given in the long answer questions on Drama, Prose and Poetry.
5. Do not exceed the prescribed word limit while answering the questions in Section B.
6. The intended marks for questions are given in brackets [ ].

Time : 3 Hrs.

Max. Marks : 80

Section A *(20 Marks)*

Question 1.

Choose the correct option for the following questions. (10)

(i) What happens when Macbeth attempts to influence his fate by murdering Banquo and Fleance? [Recall]

(a) He successfully changes his future with his efforts

(b) The witches' prophecy proves to be a trick

(c) In his efforts to control fate, he ends up sealing his own ruin

(d) He experienced success for a while but could not keep a hold on it

(ii) What is the first thing that catches Macbeth's attention when he enters the banquet? [Recall]

(a) The decorations (b) Duncan's ghost

(c) Banquo's ghost (d) Fleance hiding

(iii) What does Lady Macduff think of Macduff's reason for disappearing? [Understanding]

(a) Fear (b) Revenge

(c) Saving his own life (d) Jealousy

(iv) In Act IV, why does Macbeth say "We have scorched the snake, not killed it"? [Analysis]

(P) He was anxious as he acquired the throne by treason

(Q) He was scared of retaliation

(R) He was scared of Fleance's return

(S) He was afraid of Macduff

(a) (P) and (Q) (b) (P) and (R) (c) (Q) and (S) (d) (R) and (S)

(v) In the story 'Indigo', on which day did Aniruddha set out for his journey to Dumka? [Recall]

(a) 21st April
(b) 27th April
(c) 21st August
(d) 27th August

(vi) How did Tarapada, in the story 'Atithi', familiarise himself with the people so easily? [Understanding]

(a) He manipulated them
(b) He knew different languages
(c) He was charismatic and engaging
(d) He lured people with his words

(vii) According to the story 'The Medicine Bag', select the correct option. [Analysis]

Statement I One year Cheryl had new moccasins that Grandpa had made.

Statement II The kids ran to the curb, where they watched me and the old man.

(a) Statement I and II are the same.
(b) Statement I is a result of Statement II.
(c) Statement I and II are unrelated.
(d) Statement II is a result of statement I.

(viii) In the poem 'Telephone Conversation', how does the landlady react when the speaker doesn't give a direct answer to her question and says "West African sepia"? [Interpret]

(a) She laughs it off
(b) She gets angry
(c) She becomes curious
(d) She apologises

(ix) In the poem 'Tithonus', which literary device describes Tithonus' ageing? [Understanding]

(a) Simile (b) Irony (c) Hyperbole (d) Metaphor

(x) What is the audience's reaction to Beethoven's performance according to the poem 'Beethoven'? [Understanding]

(a) Applause (b) Tearing up (c) Whispers in awe (d) All of these

Question 2.

Complete the following sentences by providing a reason for each in brief. Do not write the question. (10)

SP-10

(i) According to Act IV of the play, Macbeth was envious of Duncan because .... [Understanding]

(ii) In Act III Scene 6 of the play, there is irony in Lennox's speech because .... [Understanding]

(iii) In Act IV of the play, Macduff's son doesn't fear anything because .... [Analysis]

(iv) In Act V, Caithness cautions that "Great Dunsinane he strongly fortifies" because .... [Analysis]

(v) Tarapada decided to leave the gymnastic group and move to Nandigram because .... [Recall]

(vi) The author strikes a sarcastic remark at the automated house in the story 'There Will Come Soft Rains', saying "...not even a bird must touch the house!" because .... [Analysis]

(vii) In the story 'Indigo', Aniruddha had decided to leave after breakfast but couldn't because .... [Recall]

(viii) In the poem 'Tithonus', the speaker appreciates mortals for their fate because .... [Understanding]

(ix) From the poem 'Beethoven', the concluding message 'Listen' is important because .... [Analysis]

(x) In the poem 'Small Towns and the River', the poetess says "A shrine of happy pictures marks the days of childhood…" because .... [Interpret]

Section B *(60 Marks)*

Macbeth-William Shakespeare

Question 3.

(i) Discuss Banquo's soliloquy at the beginning of Act III Scene 1 of *Macbeth*. Give your answer in 100-150 words including the following details. [Evaluate] (5)

(a) An insight into his thoughts

(b) The reason for suppressing his thoughts

(ii) How does Macbeth's first meeting with the murderers in Act III unravel his knavery? Give your answer in 100-150 words including the following details. [Understanding] (5)

(a) He convinced them

(b) The instructions he gave

(iii) (a) Discuss the theme of manipulation in the play *Macbeth* based on your reading of acts studied. Write your answer in 200-250 words. [Analysis] (10)

Or

(b) Based on the reading of Act V, describe how people who were on Macbeth's side, started leaving him ultimately leading him to his downfall. Write your answer in 200-250 words. [Evaluate]

Prism-A Collection of Short Stories

Question 4.

(i) In the story 'Indigo', why did Aniruddha decide to visit his friend? [Analysis] (5)

(a) Description of his journey

(b) The challenges he faced

(ii) In the story 'The Cookie Lady', why did Mrs. Drew bake cookies for Bubber? [Analysis] (5)

(a) Bubber's action when he visited her

(b) Its effect on Mrs. Drew

(iii) (a) Based on the story 'Atithi', why do you think Tarapada never stayed at one place for a long time? Do you think travelling affects a person's personality? Discuss in 200-250 words. [Evaluate] (10)

Or

(b) Based on the story 'The Medicine Bag', what do you understand about Martin's inner struggle in accepting his culture and how did he overcome it? Write your answer in 200-250 words. [Understanding]

SP-10

Rhapsody-Poetry

Question 5.

(i) What are the literary devices used in the opening lines of the poem 'Tithonus'? [Interpret] (5)
 (a) What do you infer from these lines?
 (b) The tone of the lines

(ii) In the poem 'Death Be Not Proud', why is death compared to a slave? [Analysis] (5)
 (a) Death be a slave to a king
 (b) The paradox in the last line of the poem.

(iii) (a) From the poem 'Telephone Conversation', what lines made an impression on you and why? Discuss in 200-250 words. [Recall] (10)

Or

(b) Discuss the linguistic devices employed by the poet in the lines "Beethoven's musical measurements could take you to distances...they shook the constellations..." from the poem 'Beethoven'. How do these linguistic devices create an impact on the reader and what do they inform us about Beethoven's music? Write your answer in 200-250 words. [Analysis and Evaluate]

Answers *in Topper's Style*

1. (i) (b) The witches' prophecy proves to be a trick
 (ii) (c) Banquo's ghost
 (iii) (a) Fear
 (iv) (b) (P) and (R)
 (v) (b) 27th April
 (vi) (c) He was charismatic and engaging
 (vii) (c) Statement I and II are unrelated.
 (viii) (c) She becomes curious
 (ix) (d) Metaphor
 (x) (d) All of these

2. (i) Duncan was safe from worries and thoughts of treachery
 (ii) he suspects Macbeth to be the mastermind behind the recent murders
 (iii) according to him, if he's fatherless, he must be pitiful and he gives an analogy of the birds saying hunters don't catch pitiful birds
 (iv) Macbeth is safeguarding his castle as the Lords have turned against him
 (v) he wished to join another jatra group and explore a new place
 (vi) the house's safety system protects it from all possible damage or invasion but ironically couldn't protect its inhabitants, for whom the security system was designed
 (vii) his Uncle Mohit had come to his house unannounced, and he had to stay and spend time with him till the evening
 (viii) his gift of immortality has turned into a curse for him as he keeps ageing but doesn't die, therefore he starts appreciating the natural cycle of life and death
 (ix) it emphasises the importance of listening with intent and not just hearing. The poet urges the readers to try and grasp the depth in Beethoven's music
 (x) the pictures remind us of the nostalgic memories and innocence of childhood, defining the early stages of life

3. (i) In Act III Scene 1 of the play, Banquo has a moment to himself when he expresses his concerns regarding King Duncan's murder and Macbeth's appointment as a king. He suspects Macbeth of being the executioner of the King's murder because the witches' prophecy has come true. It makes him suspicious because he knows Macbeth could have played foul and used deceit in order to make those prophecies come true. His mind wanders to think that, if whatever the witches told them was true, his son too may acquire the throne someday. However, he stops himself from thinking such things right then and suppresses his emotions as he wishes to stay

loyal to his country and, unlike Macbeth, Banquo does not let the thought of power consume him.

(ii) Macbeth's first meeting with the murderers reveals his knavery. Although he wishes to remove Banquo and Fleance from his way, he doesn't want to do it himself. Therefore, he very skillfully appeals to the murderer's ambition questioning their manhood to convince them to execute the murders of Banquo and Fleance for him. His instructions are clear as he commands them to eliminate Banquo and his son, Fleance who threaten his reign and are the cause of his crippling anxiety. The murderers, who were eager to prove themselves, carry out the deed at night, killing Banquo and leaving Macbeth's guilt and ambition intertwined. Hence, Macbeth's encounter with the murderers exposes his treacherous intentions and his hunger for power.

(iii) (a) In the play *Macbeth*, the theme of 'manipulation' is prominently highlighted as the tragedy unfolds. In Act III, Macbeth manipulates the murderers to execute Banquo's murder for him. To convince them to do his dark deeds, he manipulates them with fabricated evidence to turn them against Banquo and weaves a trail of lies. He skillfully appeals to the murderer's ambition questioning their manhood to convince them to execute the murders of Banquo and Fleance for him. Another instance showing manipulation in the play is Macbeth trying to manipulate his own 'fate'. He takes dangerous measures and even commits regicide in order to make the witches' prophecies come true and to acquire the throne of Scotland. Furthermore, manipulation is seen in other instances from the play as Hecate uses her power over the witches to manipulate them into doing what she wants and asks them to confuse Macbeth. Following her instructions, the witches manipulate Macbeth and plant seeds of ambition and lust for power by showing him the apparitions and playing with his already corrupt psyche.

To conclude, the use of these examples of manipulation in this unfolding tragedy by Shakespeare serves as a cautionary tale against unchecked desires and misuse of power.

(b) In Act V of *Macbeth*, the unravelling of Macbeth's support system and his army accelerates, culminating in his tragic downfall. First, Lady Macbeth, who was once his confidante and co-conspirator, succumbs to guilt and madness. Her sleepwalking, haunted by the blood on her hands, reveals her inner torment which ultimately drives her to death and leaves Macbeth isolated and without her strategic counsel. Then, the Scottish lords, who initially supported Macbeth, start to view him as a tyrant. They start supporting the English army's approach which is led by Malcolm. Later on, Macbeth's fury and fortification of Dunsinane Castle alienate him further. His former allies distance themselves from Macbeth recognising his tyranny. Furthermore, the prophecy that Macbeth cannot die until Birnam Wood moves to Dunsinane haunts him. When he learns that the trees of Birnam Wood are advancing towards the Dunsinane castle, he faces Macduff's invincible army. He then faces his true fate as Macduff defeats and kills him, and Malcolm ascends the throne.

In this web of betrayal, Macbeth's ambition, paranoia and ruthless actions lead to his tragic end. The very forces he manipulated to gain power turn against him leaving him isolated, desperate and ultimately defeated.

4. (i) In Satyajit Ray's short story 'Indigo', Aniruddha's childhood longing for escape from the bustling city stayed with him. When his friend Promode, who was posted at the Forest Department in Dumka, invited him to visit, Aniruddha eagerly accepted. He decided to travel to Dumka by car as he was a confident driver and the journey was two hundred miles long. He couldn't wait to get away from the city so he left as soon as he saw his uncle Mohit off who had come to visit him unannounced and delayed his departure. So, when Aniruddha started for Dumka, it was already nighttime. His journey went quite well in the beginning but as soon as he reached Panagarh military camps, he heard a bang as he got a flat tire. Soon, his journey started going downhill from there as he then encountered a thunderstorm and another flat tire. Later, he realised he had taken a wrong turn and was nowhere near Dumka. As he looked around to find a shelter for the night, he reached the Dak Bungalow and experienced something supernatural and scary that he could never forget.

(ii) In Philip K. Dick's short story 'The Cookie Lady', Mrs. Drew baked cookies for Bubber, a young boy who frequently visited her. She baked those cookies for Bubber because she knew they were his weakness and would lure him into her house. While she appeared kind and generous on the outside, by offering cookies to Bubber, she actually meant to drain Bubber's youth and vitality. Whenever Bubber visited her, he focused on eating as many cookies as he wanted and Mrs. Drew let him; in turn, she would ask him to sit next to her and read from his school books. While

Mrs. Drew sat near Bubber, she felt a jolt of energy and supernaturally turned into a young and beautiful woman from a sickly old lady and this made her wish to keep having Bubber over so that she could experience youth by draining his youthful energy.

(iii) (a) In Rabindranath Tagore's story 'Atithi', Tarapada never stayed at one place for a long time. He left his home when he was young because he had a calling to explore the world through his travels. He wandered without a terminal destination, drawn by the blissful nature and the people he encountered. His interactions with the world were transient, much like a guest who never overstays its welcome.

Tarapada wins the hearts of people through his free-spirited nature and his engaging interactions with them. His travels have instilled in him a sense of independence and a charismatic demeanour which makes him curious about life. Tarapada's stories of his adventures and his carefree attitude towards life bring a sense of excitement and novelty to the villagers' otherwise monotonous routines; therefore, he is loved wherever he goes. His ability to connect with people from all walks of life, coupled with his youthful exuberance, allows him to form genuine bonds with the villagers leaving a lasting impression on their hearts.

It is a well-known fact that extended travel can alter an individual's traits. When we explore unfamiliar territories, we gain new perspectives and appreciate diversity. Travel fosters openness to experience, emotional stability and self-confidence. Stepping out of our comfort zone exposes us to different cultures, challenging our preconceptions and broadening our horizons. As travellers, we adapt to unexpected changes realising that life's journey matters more than the destination itself. Therefore, travelling changes one's personality and their way of seeing and experiencing the world.

(b) In 'The Medicine Bag' by Virginia Driving Hawk Sneve, Martin grapples with an inner conflict related to his cultural identity. Martin, a teenage boy of mixed heritage, feels embarrassed by his grandfather's unexpected visit. He fears that his friends will discover his Grandpa's presence and will want to meet him which would shatter the fantastical image he has carefully crafted about him through his stories. Martin's modern identity clashes with the traditional and mystical aura surrounding his grandfather. Martin loves his grandfather but is hesitant to introduce him to his friends as he does not look like the typical native Indians that are shown in the media. However, as the story progresses and his friends eventually meet his Grandpa, Martin feels ashamed of his own feelings as his friends are impressed by Grandpa and do not laugh at him for being exotic.

Later on, when Grandpa explains the history and significance of his medicine bag to him, he feels proud of his roots. Ultimately, Martin accepts his mixed identity with love and respect. After his grandfather's passing, he even wears the medicine bag appreciating the symbolism of his connection to his culture and his ancestors. In essence, Martin's journey from embarrassment to acceptance reflects the importance of family heritage and the need to embrace traditions with love and respect.

5. (i) Alfred, Lord Tennyson has employed many literary devices in the opening lines of his poem 'Tithonus'. First is the imagery. The lines vividly describe the decay of the woods, the weeping vapours, and the cycle of life and death. The imagery evokes a sense of impermanence and melancholy. Second is the repetition. The repetition of 'the woods decay' emphasises the relentless passage of time and mortality. From these lines, we understand that Tithonus, unlike natural elements, cannot die. He longs for mortality desiring release from eternal ageing. His immortality becomes a curse to him, consuming him slowly. Hence, he yearns for the ordinary fate of mortals. The tone is sombre, reflective and introspective. Tithonus's lamentation reveals his weariness and regret. The lines convey a sense of resignation and longing emphasising the tragic irony of his immortal existence.

(ii) In John Donne's poem 'Death Be Not Proud', the comparison of death to a slave serves as a powerful metaphor. The speaker asserts that death is not a master but a slave. It is subject to external forces including fate, chance and even kings. Kings, who wield power over life and death, can command death to take lives. Thus, death becomes subservient to their authority.

The poem concludes with the paradoxical statement: 'And death shall be no more; Death, thou shalt die'. This paradox lies in the contradiction that if, death dies, how can it continue to exist? The very concept of death ceasing to be contradicts its nature. Symbolically, it suggests that death, despite its apparent power, ultimately loses its dominion. According to the poet, eternal life transcends death, rendering death powerless.

(iii) (a) In Wole Soyinka's poem 'Telephone Conversation', several lines leave a lasting impact revealing the complexities of racial prejudice and hypocrisy.

The opening line 'The price seemed reasonable, location indifferent' sets the scene for a seemingly mundane conversation about renting an apartment. However, it hints at deeper issues where the price and location matter less than the speaker's identity. The word 'indifferent' clearly suggests that the landlady's attitude toward location is nonchalant but her attitude toward race may not be. Then, the phrase 'wasted journey' implies that the speaker has faced rejection before due to his race, making him wary.

Additionally, the most impactful line of all - 'HOW DARK? . . . ARE YOU LIGHT OR VERY DARK?' - where the landlady's abrupt question to the speaker exposes her racial bias as she wants to categorise the speaker based on his skin colour. This highlights the presence of racial prejudice and how people are not hesitant in expressing it to people who look different from them.

There are other such lines in the poem, which collectively expose the absurdity of racial discrimination. The poem masterfully uses irony and satire to critique societal biases turning a mundane phone call into a powerful commentary on human interactions across racial lines.

(b) In the lines quoted from the poem 'Beethoven', the poet employs several linguistic devices to evoke a vivid and impactful experience for the reader. The phrase 'musical measurements' contains consonance, specifically the repetition of the 'm' sound. This repetition creates a musical quality in the language itself emphasising the theme of music. It draws attention to the precision and intricacy of Beethoven's compositions as if each note was meticulously measured and calculated.

Furthermore, in 'Take you to distances', the word 'distances' creates imagery of vastness and exploration. Beethoven's music transcends physical boundaries transporting listeners to emotional and imaginative realms. Similarly, in 'Shook the constellations', the poet uses cosmic imagery. The constellations represent the celestial order and Beethoven's music disrupts this order. It suggests that his compositions have cosmic impact, shaking the very fabric of the universe. The word 'shook' implies both power and disruption.

There is also the use of metaphor in 'Musical measurements'. This metaphorical phrase implies that Beethoven's music isn't merely notes on a staff rather it is a precise measurement of emotions, experiences and human existence.

It suggests that music is a universal language that can quantify the ineffable. Through the use of these linguistic devices, poet has made these lines memorable and evocative for the reader. The use of these strong metaphors also tells us that Beethoven's compositions are more than mere notes; they are profound expressions of human emotion and experience.

Knowledge Booster Zone

Welcome to the Knowledge Booster Zone !

This section is dedicated to enhancing your understanding of key ideas associated with the stories, poems and drama.

Here, you will find chapter-wise quick study notes designed to solidify your **foundational knowledge**. Use these notes to review and reinforce what you've learned, ensuring you're well-prepared to answer the questions.

Progress Tracker Tick the chapters as you revise them.

Prose

- ☐ Atithi (Guest)
- ☐ There Will Come Soft Rains
- ☐ The Medicine Bag
- ☐ The Cookie Lady
- ☐ Indigo

Poetry

- ☐ Telephone Conversation
- ☐ Beethoven
- ☐ Death Be Not Proud
- ☐ Tithonus
- ☐ Small Towns and the River

Drama

- ☐ Macbeth
  - Act III
  - Act IV
  - Act V

Chapter I Atithi (Guest) by Rabindranath Tagore

Setting
This story is set in the rural area of Bengal in the nineteenth century.

Important Characters
Tarapada-protagonist, Motilal Babu-the kind zamindar, Annapurna-Motilal Babu's wife, Charushashi- Motilal Babu's daughter, Sonamani- a child widow, Charushashi's friend.

Theme
Nature, Learning through experiences, Pursuit of a meaningful life, Freedom, Human nature.

- 'Atithi' is a short story about a young Brahmin boy of fifteen years of age, named Tarapada, who is fascinated by nature and loves to travel, explore new places and learn new skills.
- He's naturally loved by everyone he meets due to his charismatic demeanour and charming personality.
- In the story, Tarapada runs away from home at a very young age without informing anyone and joins a yatra/jatra-troupe.
- Despite having a loving family and neighbourhood, he keeps running away from home. He craves to be one with nature and to be able to see the world so he chooses to be a wanderer.
- Therefore, after his several attempts of running away from home, his family eventually gives up on trying to keep him at the same place.
- He goes on to join several other troupes and learns to do various things like playing a flute selling things and taking care of himself.
- One day, he meets a zamindar, Motilal Babu, who was travelling to Kathaliya village by a boat with his wife Annapurna and daughter Charushashi.
- He asked Motilal Babu for a lift to the village Nandigram which was on the way to Kathaliya; so, he agreed and invited Tarapada to his boat with kindness due to his innocent appearance and charming personality.
- Tarapada was treated with motherly love and hospitality by Annapurna and he too, without any hesitation, started helping out with various chores like cooking, shopping and sailing the boat.
- On a fine evening, when Motilal Babu was reading out Ramayan to his wife and daughter, Tarapada couldn't help but join them. He started playing the flute which mesmerised everyone even the neighbouring boats.
- Tarapada was highly praised but Charushashi did not like it and grew jealous of Tarapada.
- Charushashi, being the only child, was not happy with sharing her parents' affections with anyone else and, when she saw everyone praising Tarapada for his many talents, she started being even more difficult than she already was and threw tantrums about anything and everything, troubling her parents.
- Soon, they crossed Nandigram and Tarapada did not even notice it. Along with Motilal Babu's family, he came to the village Kathaliya and instantly established relations with the whole village calling them 'dada', 'khura' or 'masi'. He was wholeheartedly welcomed by the village.
- Tarapada's calm nature and friendly attitude towards everyone made him everyone's favourite.
- Charushashi, on the other hand, kept hovering between jealousy, envy, hatred and gentleness towards Tarapada. Even though she did not admit it, she developed a liking towards Tarapada and thought of her family as the only claimants of Tarapada.
- Therefore, one day when her friend, Sonamani, a child widow, visited her, Charushashi told her about Tarapada but to her surprise Sonamani and her mother were already familiar with him.

- *Tarapada called Sonamani's mother 'masi' and Sonamani called him 'Dada'. This infuriated Charushashi and she started pushing Sonamani away whenever she came to visit her and threw more tantrums at Tarapada to get his attention.*
- *However, Tarapada was intrigued by Charushashi's behaviour and the rift between their contrasting natures continued.*
- *Contrary to Tarapada's nature, he decided to stay in Kathaliya for a while.*
- *Seeing Tarapada's fascination with books, Motilal Babu hired an English tutor for him. This quenched Tarapada's thirst for knowledge and he dedicatedly gave all his concentration and time to his academic endeavours.*
- *Two years passed and Tarapada had not left the village. Meanwhile, Charushashi turned eleven and her father arranged matches to get her married. However, Charushashi did not take any restrictions and couldn't be convinced to behave when the family of the boy came to see her.*
- *Therefore, Annapurna suggested that they arrange her marriage with Tarapada who they know well and will stay with them. This will allow them to stay close to their only daughter during old age.*
- *After much thought and running a thorough background check on Tarapada's family, Motilal Babu fixed Tarapada and Charushashi's wedding in the month of Sraban.*
- *Invitation to Tarapada's family was sent and all the arrangements were made for the wedding but Motilal Babu did not inform Tarapada about any of it.*
- *Tarapada, drawn to the hustle-bustle, went to see the famous chariot-festival at the Nag Estate, at Kurulkata, on the evening before the wedding.*
- *The next morning, Tarapada's family arrived at Kathaliya village but Tarapada was nowhere to be seen. He had once again left stealing everyone's heart and breaking all the ties before they could encircle him.*

Values Imparted

- This story shows the beauty of our spiritual connection with nature which frees us from all kinds of bonds. From the story, we also learn how one can learn from every opportunity that life presents and develop through experiences.

Chapter 2 The Cookie Lady by Philip K. Dick

Setting
The story is set in a small neighbourhood and has an eerie tone to it.

Important Characters
Bubber (Bernard) Surle- a young boy, Mrs. Drew- a strange old lady in the neighbourhood, May Surle and Ralf Surle- Bubber's parents, Ernie Mill- Bubber's classmate.

Themes
Exploitation of innocence, Consequences of negligence, Greed, loneliness.

- *This story is about a young boy named Bernard Surle (Bubber) who likes to visit the very old Mrs. Drew living in his neighbourhood.*
- *The story begins with Bubber on his way to see Mrs. Drew when his friend Ernie Mill mocks him for frequently visiting the old lady.*
- *Although Mrs. Drew had an eerie presence about her and was known as the 'creepy old lady' in the neighbourhood, her demeanour around Bubber appeared to be kind.*
- *Bubber used to pass by her house and Mrs. Drew hoped to get his attention by offering him freshly baked cookies.*

- *Bubber, being a child, loved cookies. He easily surrendered to his craving and went inside the house.*
- *Since then, for a month, she would bake him fresh cookies each day and ask him to read to her to spend more time in his company.*
- *Her intentions although were not clear but something strange happened whenever Bubber sat near Mrs. Drew reading from his school books.*
- *Mrs. Drew began to change supernaturally into a beautiful young woman, her wrinkles disappeared and her cheeks became fuller. She felt youthful again.*
- *But, this change only lasted as long as Bubber stayed in the house. She returned to her frail looking self as soon as he left.*
- *However, Bubber, on the other hand, felt exhausted whenever he came home after visiting Mrs. Drew. Noticing this, Bubber's parents grew concerned and forbade him from visiting the strange old lady.*
- *Bubber decides to visit Mrs. Drew one last time so he goes to her house and as always she has the cookies baked ready for him. When Bubber tells her that this would be his last visit to her, she grows sad and sits next to him as he eats and reads to her.*
- *This time, she touches Bubber's arm and feels his youth flowing into her like energy and she transforms into a young woman again. But this time, it doesn't go away and she happily plans to go out.*
- *Bubber, on the contrary, feels tired and weak on his way home. His parents worry about him when he doesn't return and the weather starts getting bad.*
- *When they check outside the house, they only see a bundle of weeds and rags blowing with the wind and Bubber is nowhere to be found.*

Values Imparted

- The story highlights the consequences of not keeping our desires in check. Through Bubber's example, we learn that we should not let our 'greed' dictate our choices in life.

Chapter 3 There Will Come Soft Rains by Ray Bradbury

Setting

The story is set in 2026 describing the world after a nuclear blast during 'War Time'.

Important Characters

The central character of the story is an automated house and the story has no human characters.

Themes

Nature vs. technology, Restoration of balance by nature.

- *The story begins with the voice-clock in the living room of the empty-automated-house blaring out the morning alarm and reading out event reminders for the day.*
- *There is no sign of any human activity or the inhabitants in the house but the house still runs on a set programme and performs its duties diligently.*
- *The intricate mechanical setup of the house runs all the utility equipment and performs its daily functions like the stove cooking breakfast, serving it and even washing the dishes.*
- *The weather box singing and alerting for rain, the garage door opening and shutting, the tiny robotic mice whirring around the house cleaning every dust particle that comes in their way and the sprinklers watering the lawn, all in a timely manner.*

- *In the afternoon the dog owned by the family who had lived in the house returns at its door, shivering and covered with many injuries. It leaves trails of mud as he goes inside the house in search of his owners and food, but finds nothing.*
- *The automated kitchen starts preparing pancakes, the smell of which, makes the dog scratch at the glass door greedily but it doesn't open. The dog soon dies and its remains are cleaned up by the robotic mice within fifteen minutes.*
- *Later in the afternoon, the house continues to follow its routine and prepares various things like the card game at the patio and the colourful show of fake animals in the children's nursery.*
- *In the evening, the house selects a random poem 'There Will Come Soft Rains by Sara Teasdale' for the mother of the family.*
- *Ironically, the poem is about wartime and describes how the world would be if mankind perished and nature would still restore its balance and carry on.*
- *After sometime the wind blows and a branch of a tree falls off into the house and causes the house to catch fire.*
- *The safety system of the house responds by turning the sprinklers on but nothing helps and slowly the whole house gets consumed by the fierce fire.*
- *At the end, only a wall and one mechanical voice remains which keeps saying "Today is August 5, 2026..." repeatedly.*

Values Imparted

- This story warns humans on their mindless use of technology and their complete reliance on it. It also tells us, that nature's balance and peace is the only lasting element, and it is indifferent to selfish human ways.

Chapter 4 Indigo by Satyajit Ray

Setting	Important Characters	Themes
This story has a post-colonial setting, in the urban area of Bengal and Jharkhand, mainly around the city of Calcutta (Kolkata) and district Dumka.	Aniruddha Bose- protagonist and narrator, uncle Mohit- Aniruddha's uncle, Bhola Babu- Aniruddha's neighbour, Promode- Aniruddha's friend, Sukhanram- the man who helps Aniruddha, caretaker of the Dak Bungalow.	Fantasy, Horror and Adventure.

- *Aniruddha Bose sets off on a tragic car ride that takes unexpected turns and finally brings him to the unsettling Dak Bungalow in Satyajit Ray's creepy short story 'Indigo'.*
- *Twenty-nine-year-old Aniruddha, a bachelor employed at an advertising agency, makes the decision to pay his friend Promode a visit in Dumka.*
- *Initially, he gets late in starting his journey due to his uncle's (uncle Mohit) unexpected visit and is later on faced by queries from his neighbour, Bhola Babu who thinks driving for two hundred miles at night is not a good idea.*
- *Unfazed by the initial delays and halts, he begins his journey but soon encounters the first challenge as his car's tyre bursts.*
- *Then, after some time, he gets stuck in a thunderstorm.*

- *Once more, fate steps in, causing another tyre to rupture during the storm. Aniruddha discovers he has made a wrong turn and can't move ahead as his car needs another change of tyre and there was no sign of any shops nearby.*
- *He is left all alone on the road, in a car that won't move, in the middle of the night.*
- *In desperation, he sees what appears to be a light in a window at a distance.*
- *Pulling out his torch, he finds an old man named Sukhanram, who offers him shelter in the Dak Bungalow. Aniruddha learns that the bungalow once belonged to an English sahib who was an indigo planter.*
- *The nearby factory's chimney stands as a lonely figure. That night, strange occurrences unfold such as scratching at the door, a missing wristwatch, and a vanished suitcase.*
- *Aniruddha's hands turn pale, his voice changes, and his clothes and surroundings change too.*
- *He feels possessed by the spirit of the greedy planter and experiences a chilling transformation.*
- *Ultimately, Aniruddha's car journey to Dumka turns into a supernatural adventure with interesting twists and turns.*

Values Imparted

- The lesson that we can learn from this story is that, in life, things don't go according to our plans all the time, but we must embrace its uncertainty as it might surprise us and take us on an unexpected adventure.

Chapter 5 The Medicine Bag by Virginia Driving Hawk Sneve

Setting

The story is set in the city of Iowa and the native land of Rosebud Reservation in South Dakota, in America.

Important Characters

Martin- a young boy, the protagonist and narrator, Grandpa- Martin's maternal grandfather, Native Indian belonging to the Sioux tribe, Cheryl- Martin's sister, Marie- Martin's mother.

Themes

Struggle of cultural assimilation, Importance of culture and identity.

- *This story is about a teenage boy named Martin, who belongs to the Native American land of South Dakota, and his relationship with his heritage and culture.*
- *Martin's family lives in the city while his grandfather stays in the Rosebud Reservation in South Dakota.*
- *One day, Martin is caught by surprise when he goes outside the house to check what caused the stir-up and chaos in the street, and finds his Grandpa walking towards him.*
- *He feels conscious to see his Grandpa in the city as his appearance does not match the fantastical stories that he has told his friends about his grandfather.*
- *Martin loves his Grandpa but feels embarrassed of him as he does not reflect the image of Native Indians that city people have in their minds due to their exaggerated portrayal on TV.*
- *However, he instantly feels a regret for his feelings of embarrassment when he sees his sister Cheryl and his mother happily welcoming him.*
- *When their friends learn of Grandpa's presence, Cheryl and Martin have opposite reactions.*
- *Cheryl's friends frequently visit Grandpa as they love his warm demeanour and his interesting stories; however, Martin keeps avoiding his friends and makes excuses.*
- *One day, despite Martin's reluctance, his friends accompany him to his house after school, to meet his Grandpa and to his surprise, they all find him fascinating, which makes Martin regret his initial emotions.*

- *Later on, Grandpa explains the importance of the medicine bag that he always carries with him to Martin which helps him appreciate his culture.*
- *By spending more time with Grandpa, Martin's feelings change about his identity and he embraces his cultural heritage.*
- *As the rightful male heir, he accepts the medicine bag when Grandpa dies.*

Values Imparted

- Through this story we learn that we must not judge a book by its cover as Martin was worried about his friends not liking Grandpa due to his appearance but he was wrong. The story also urges us to learn about our culture and embrace it proudly.

Poetry

Chapter 1 Telephone Conversation by Wole Soyinka

Setting

The setting of the poem is in an unnamed country, implied to be England in the twentieth century. The conversation in the poem takes place in a red telephone booth.

Important Characters

The speaker- an African man looking for an apartment, The landlady- a polite but judgemental won.

Themes

Racial discrimination and prejudice.

- *As the title suggests, this poem is about a telephonic interaction between an African man and a British landlady. The landlady initially appears pleasant but her demeanour changes abruptly when the speaker reveals he is African.*
- *Although she had advertised the room without racial restrictions, her true feelings emerge as soon as she learns about the speaker's background.*
- *Throughout the poem, the poet masterfully employs irony and satire.*
- *The mundane act of seeking accommodation becomes an example of societal prejudice.*
- *The speaker cleverly navigates the conversation and uses humour to bring out the ridiculousness of the landlady's question about his skin colour.*
- *The speaker tells her that his skin is as dark as "West African Sepia" and begins to state the colours of each part of his body.*
- *The poem satirises racial discrimination.*
- *The poet has emphasised on the absurdity of racist attitudes and exposed its prevalence in the society despite having laws against it.*
- *The poem brings out human follies, the racial discrimination, the hatred towards black people in the society, in a sarcastic tone.*

Values Imparted

- The poem highlights the persistent discrimination in the society but, through the speaker's attitude and clever navigation of the conversation, we can learn that it is our attitude towards a situation that dictates in which direction it may turn.

Chapter 2 Tithonus by Alfred, Lord Tennyson

Setting

This poem is set in the celestial palace of Goddess Aurora/Eos where she holds court.

Important Characters

Tithonus- the speaker, Aurora's lover, Aurora/Eos- Goddess of dawn.

Theme

Old age and death, unchecked human desires.

- *The poem is a dramatic monologue by Tithonus who is the speaker in the poem. He is the lover of Aurora, Goddess of dawn.*
- *Tithonus laments that while the old leaves fall off the trees and men who work in the fields grow old and die, he is cursed to live forever.*
- *Tithonus tells Aurora that he was once a beautiful man and now he is like a grey shadow in her arms.*
- *When he asked Aurora to give him immortality, she granted his wish without thinking of the consequences.*
- *Tithonus says that he angered the Hours (Goddesses who accompany Aurora) by accepting the gift of immortality and they took revenge on him by making him old and withered.*
- *Now, Tithonus is forced to live each day in suffering while Aurora renews her youth each day and stays young.*
- *Tithonus regrets his choice of wanting to be different from other mortals and realises the value of the natural cycle of life and death.*
- *He requests Aurora to take back her gift but she leaves before she could fulfil his request and, sometimes, it scares him when she looks at him with a tearful look.*
- *He wonders if the old saying about Gods not being able to recall their gift is true.*
- *Tithonus sighs and reminisces the past memories of his youth and how he enjoyed being young and in love.*
- *He asks Aurora to not keep him 'imprisoned' in the East where she rises and becomes new each day and his old age, in sharp contrast with her youth, torments him even more.*
- *He requests her to grant him death so that she can look at his grave each morning and he doesn't have to bear the sting of her silver wheels.*

Values Imparted

- This poem serves as a cautionary tale. It warns against unchecked human desires. The poem even suggests that the embrace of death is a kind of wisdom that only comes with age. The arrogant young Tithonus could never have imagined wanting his life to be over; however, all that the elderly Tithonus wishes for, is death.

Chapter 3 Beethoven by Shane Koyczan

Setting	Important Characters	Themes
This poem does not have a defined setting.	Beethoven- the artist, Beethoven's father.	Tribute to the art and the artist, tribute to Ludwig van Beethoven

- *The poem 'Beethoven' revolves around the struggles of a young boy who struggles with emotional and physical limitations, and abuse, while trying to achieve mastery in his art of music.*
- *The poem begins and ends with the word 'Listen' which emphasises on the idea that to understand Beethoven's music, one must make a point of 'listening with intent'.*
- *Growing up in a household that doesn't offer love and support, and his father's constant beating shaped Beethoven's determination to excel in music.*
- *Despite being deaf, Beethoven learnt to make compositions on his piano by breaking the legs of his piano and feeling its vibrations through the floor.*
- *No matter how softly or swiftly he played, to his father, it was 'never good enough'.*
- *The phrase 'Not good enough' is repeatedly used by the poet to emphasise the impact these words had on the young child's mind.*
- *When he grows older and performs, the audiences are thrilled by the sound of his magical symphonies.*
- *His dedication to his craft is remarkable.*
- *However, he can't hear their applause or their whispers in awe and fails to acknowledge how much his music is loved by his audience.*
- *Due to never receiving praise for his music from his father, Beethoven too never praised any of his fellow instrumentalists.*
- *Through the use of vivid imagery in the poem and the emotional depth in his delivery, the poet has paid a tribute to the great artist of all times, Beethoven.*

Values Imparted

- This poem teaches us the value of persistence. Through persistence and hard work, Beethoven defeated all his limitations and came to be known as one of the world's best composers.

Chapter 4 Small Towns and the River by Mamang Dai

Setting	Important Characters	Themes
The poem is set in a small town by the river situated in the midst of trees.	There are no specific characters in the poem.	Life and death, Nature, Spirituality, Eternity.

- *The poem 'Small Towns and the River' is a metaphorical description of the cycle of life, death and spirituality.*
- *In this poem the poetess has given a vivid description of her small but beautiful town.*
- *The scenery of the town rarely changes, be it summer or winter, the dusty winds always blow through its valleys.*
- *It is nestled in silence amidst the trees and by a river.*
- *The poetess imagines that sometimes, the river may long for something more and hold its breath as it looks for a new land full of fish and stars.*
- *The poetess highlights the impermanence of human life by talking about the recent death in the town.*
- *As the whole town mourns the death in silence, she realises that only rituals are permanent which passed down generations.*
- *She then focuses on the river which becomes a metaphor that embodies a 'soul' and deeply understands the town's cycles.*
- *The water in the river flows constantly and is aware of its immortality.*
- *The poem also talks about the rituals regarding death and how the dead are placed pointing West anticipating the soul's journey to the East, the house of the Sun.*
- *Everyone in the small town by the river wants to walk with God.*
- *The poem ends with talking about how just like the coolness of bamboo, the Sunlight restores the peace of the soul in the body, and this is when life is of the greatest importance.*

Values Imparted

- The poem teaches us about the community values that bring people closer.

Chapter 5 Death Be Not Proud by John Donne

Setting	Important Characters	Themes
The setting of the poem is not defined.	The speaker, Death.	Eternity, Soul can't be corrupted by death, Afterlife, Death not having any power.

- *This poem is a sonnet written by John Donne in which he personifies death and addresses it directly to emphasise on its powerlessness.*
- *Through this poem, the poet challenges the conventional fear of death.*
- *The opening lines of the poem begin with the poet telling death to not be proud as it has no authority of its own.*
- *The poet says that it is mere 'fear' of death that makes death so intimidating for people.*
- *Then, he continues to compare death with a restful sleep. He says death may even be more pleasurable than sleep or rest.*
- *According to the poet's understanding, the best people get to experience death and their souls travel to the afterlife through death. Thus, death is merely a portal to the afterlife.*
- *He further makes a comparison of death with the effects induced by certain drugs and criticises death for having unnecessary pride as it can easily be controlled by people who are desperate, by luck, the kings who have power to command death and even illnesses that cause it.*
- *Hence, the poet declares death powerless and says death is nothing but a form of sleep, a phase between life on earth and heaven.*
- *It doesn't have a final say on human lives.*

Values Imparted

- Through this poem, the poet makes us realise the importance of acceptance by accepting 'death' as a natural part of our eternal soul's journey.

Macbeth Drama

Setting

William Shakespeare's Macbeth is set mainly in eleventh-century Scotland with a couple of short scenes set in England. The titular character Macbeth is a tyrant who reigned over Scotland from 1040 to 1057. It is the only play Shakespeare set in Scotland.

Important Characters

Three Witches- the Weird Sisters.

Duncan- honest and powerful man, king of Scotland.

Malcolm- Duncan's elder son.

Donalbain- Duncan's younger son.

Macbeth- protagonist, thane of Glamis who becomes king of Scotland, usurper.

Lady Macbeth- Macbeth's wife, his supporter, ambitious woman.

Three Murderers in Macbeth's service.

Banquo- commander of Scottish army, Macbeth's friend.

Fleance- Banquo's son.

Macduff- a Scottish noble.

Lady Macduff- Macduff's wife.

Siward- commander of the English forces.

Young Siward- Siward's son.

Hecate- The Goddess of dark world.

Themes

Act III – Fear, Guilt, Retribution, Political instability

Act IV – Loyalty, Fear.

Act V – Guilt, Consequences of unchecked desires, Delusion.

Act III

Scene I

- *The scene begins with Banquo delivering a soliloquy while suspecting Macbeth's ascension to the throne and the prophecy of the weird sisters (the witches) coming true.*
- *He thinks that their other prophecies will also come true where Banquo's sons become kings.*
- *But, Banquo immediately suppresses his thoughts due to his pressing conscience and honesty.*
- *Macbeth enters dressed as king and his wife, Lady Macbeth (now a queen) too follows.*
- *They invite Banquo to their celebratory banquet and Macbeth mentions that they need to discuss the matter of Malcolm and Donalbain who are sons of the dead king Duncan and have fled the country.*
- *Banquo leaves and before leaving confirms to attend the banquet with his son Fleance.*
- *Macbeth hires two murderers and makes arrangements for the killing of Banquo and Fleance.*

Scene 2

- *As the murderers hired by Macbeth make their way to Banquo, Macbeth and his wife have a brief meeting.*
- *Lady Macbeth attempts to calm Macbeth's troubled mind but ironically feels the same doubts herself.*
- *Killing the king has made them even more anxious than they had anticipated.*
- *Lady Macbeth gets shocked when Macbeth reveals his plan to murder Banquo and Fleance during the banquet.*

Scene 3

- The two murderers are joined by a third one and they wait together for Banquo at the wooded park.
- Banquo gets attacked, urges his son to flee and, thus, Fleance escapes the deadly attack.
- The murderers leave to inform Macbeth of Banquo's murder and Fleance's escape.

Scene 4

- Macbeth and Lady Macbeth welcome the Thanes of Scotland at their banquet.
- Right before the feast begins, one murderer informs Macbeth of Banquo's death and Fleance's murder.
- Macbeth praises them for their work and returns to the banquet.
- He propels between fits of courage and fear as he sees Banquo's ghost sitting at the table and mocking him.
- Lady Macbeth tries to distract the guests but eventually has to send them away as Macbeth's mind doesn't stabilise.
- Macbeth plans to murder Macduff as well as he becomes paranoid at the thought of losing the throne.
- To know more about his fate, he decides to visit the witches once again.

Scene 5

- The weird sisters (the witches) are visited by Hecate, the goddess of the dark mystic world who warns them of Macbeth's arrival.
- She reprimands them for helping Macbeth without her permission.
- She decides to play her part in his downfall and asks the witches to confuse him further.
- This scene differs in writing style from other scenes and is thought to be someone else's writing and not Shakespeare's.

Scene 6

- Lennox, the young lord that attends to Macbeth grows suspicious of Macbeth's activities.
- He discusses Macbeth's killing of Duncan's guards in a sarcastic manner, sharing his suspicions with other like-minded lords.
- One of the lords responds with news of Macduff's flight to England to seek help in overthrowing Macbeth.

Act IV

Scene I

- Macbeth visits the witches again and commands them to show him his future.
- The witches show him a series of apparitions which are horrifying in nature.
- The first apparition appears as the disembodied head of a warrior who seems to warn Macbeth of a bloody revenge by Macduff.
- The second apparition is a blood-covered child who comforts Macbeth with the news that he cannot be killed by any man born of a woman.
- The third apparition appears to be a child wearing a crown, who promises that Macbeth cannot lose in any battle until Birnam wood starts moving towards Dunsinane castle.
- Thrilled by these possibilities, Macbeth urges the witches to show him more of his future.
- In the last apparition, he sees the procession of eight crowned kings walking by, followed by one who carries a mirror.
- It is Banquo's ghost that walks at the end of the line.

- *Macbeth demands to know the meaning of the final apparition, which worries him, but the witches perform a dance and disappear leaving Macbeth confused.*
- *Lennox enters and reports to Macbeth that Macduff has fled to England.*
- *Macbeth aims to send murderers to Macduff's castle and to kill Macduff's family.*

Scene 2

- *Lady Macduff is upset with Macduff's departure.*
- *She is worried about her family's protection in the absence of their father.*
- *She aggressively addresses Ross and demands to know the reason for Macduff's running away.*
- *Ross tries to calm her down and argues that Macduff must have had a plan behind his escape as he is a wise and noble man.*
- *He also tries to warn her of the approaching danger, and asks her to run away and hide but Lady Macduff does not listen to him and stays in protest.*
- *Ross leaves and Lady Macduff turns to her son and tells him that his father is dead.*
- *Macbeth's murderers enter the room and kill Macduff's son.*
- *Lady Macduff runs away screaming and is chased by murderers.*

Scene 3

- *Macduff meets Malcolm at the English court and urges him to attack Macbeth and claim the throne as its rightful heir.*
- *Malcolm weaves a web of lies to test Macduff's loyalty as he does not trust him initially.*
- *However, Macduff's arguments convince Malcolm that he is honest and is not one of Macbeth's agents.*
- *With King Edward's help and support, Malcolm and Macduff prepare to attack the Dunsinane Castle where Macbeth is.*
- *Then, Ross arrives with the news of Macduff's family's murder by Macbeth's orders.*
- *At first, Macduff is struck with grief but soon turns it into his motivation to avenge his family's murder.*

Act V

Scene 1

- *This scene is set at the Dunsinane castle.*
- *At night, a gentlewoman, who attends to Lady Macbeth, tells the doctor that Lady Macbeth has developed a strange habit of sleepwalking.*
- *They both wait and observe her at night as she walks around with a candle and tries to wash off blood from her hands.*
- *Lady Macbeth is regretting her actions which caused the murders of Banquo and Macduff's family. Her inner turmoil is now surfacing as this new habit.*
- *The doctor says that she needs spiritual help rather than medical as her condition concerns not her body but her mind.*

Scene 2

- *Outside the castle, the Scottish lords who have turned against Macbeth discuss the situation of the army.*
- *The English army, led by Malcolm, approaches them and they all meet near the Birnam wood.*
- *They decide to join forces and attack the Dunsinane castle together which has been fortified by Macbeth.*

- Macbeth is furious and proactively makes preparations with his army, to secure himself.

Scene 3

- Macbeth walks in the halls of Dunsinane as he receives the reports about Malcolm and the English army preparing to attack him.
- However, Macbeth boasts drawing his confidence from the apparitions shown by the witches that he has nothing to worry about as he can't be killed by "any man born of woman" or "till the Birnam wood Moves".
- Then, he is informed about the number of English soldiers standing against him and he insists on putting his armour on as he wants to be prepared to fight.
- Then, the doctor comes in to inform him of Lady Macbeth's condition. He tells Macbeth that she can't be cured as her thoughts are what trouble her and not an illness.
- Macbeth feels concerned about Lady Macbeth's condition and orders the doctor to cure her condition.

Scene 4

- Malcolm discusses his attack strategy with the English soldiers and orders them to hide themselves by cutting off a branch from the tree and carry it in front of them as they march so that they can conceal their numbers.

Scene 5

- Macbeth, inside the castle, orders his officers and gets his banners hung.
- He feels confident that his castle can easily withstand any attack and he is safe.
- Suddenly, he hears a scream of a lady and he is informed of Lady Macbeth's death.
- Macbeth goes numb with shock and compares life to a 'walking shadow'. He declares life 'signifies nothing'.
- Another messenger enters and informs him that the Birnam wood is seemingly moving towards the castle.
- Macbeth suddenly recalls the witches' prophecy associated with the moving of Birnam wood.
- Desperate and in fear, he decides to abandon the castle and to die fighting the battle against Malcolm.

Scene 6

- Malcolm arrives outside the Dunsinane castle with his soldiers.
- He orders them to throw away the branches and draw their swords.
- The battle begins.

Scene 7

- On the battlefield, Macbeth kills the son of the English commander Siward.
- Full of rage and confidence that he can't be killed by any man born of a woman, he attacks and kills everyone in front of him.
- Macduff desperately looks for Macbeth as he wishes to kill him personally and avenge his family's murders.
- On the other hand, Malcolm, alongwith Siward, enters the castle and Macbeth is overthrown as the castle is surrendered to Malcolm.

Scene 8

- *Macbeth encounters Macduff on the battlefield and they begin to fight.*
- *Macbeth boasts of his power and makes Macduff aware of the witches' prophecy about being invincible. He tells Macduff that he can't be defeated as no man born of a woman can ever kill Macbeth.*
- *Macduff replies, shattering Macbeth's confidence and his delusion, that he was prematurely 'ripped' out of his mother's womb and, hence, is not 'born' of a woman.*
- *Macbeth fears for his life but doesn't surrender and gets slain by Macduff.*
- *Macduff cuts off Macbeth's head and declares Malcolm the King of Scotland.*
- *Ross informs Siward of his son's death.*
- *Malcolm declares that all the 'Thanes' will be promoted to the ranks of 'Earl' as per the English government system for the first time in the history of Scotland and expresses his gratitude to his friends and his people.*
- *He invites everyone to see him get crowned at Scone (a place in Scotland).*

Values Imparted

- The play *Macbeth*, with its various themes and characters, teaches us to not get influenced into doing something that we do not wish to do or find morally incorrect. It also emphasises on the consequences of greedy choices.